Jadite

An Identification
& Price Guide

Joe Keller & David Ross

Schiffer Publishing Ltd

4880 Lower Valley Road, Atglen, PA 19310 USA

Dedication

We would like to dedicate this book to Janet Keller and Joseph Keller Sr. for their love and support.

Copyright © 1999 by Joe Keller & David Ross.
Library of Congress Catalog Card Number: 99-62480

Design by Blair Loughrey
Type set in Horatio D Bol/Goudy Olst BT/Zapf Humanist Bt/Zurich

ISBN: 0-7643-0929-3
Printed in China
1234

748
.2913

Kell

Published by Schiffer Publishing Ltd.
4880 Lower Valley Road
Atglen, PA 19310
Phone: (610) 593-1777; Fax: (610) 593-2002
Please visit out web site catalog at
www.schifferbooks.com
or write for a free catalog.
This book may be purchased from the publisher.
Please include $3.95 for shipping.

In Europe, Schiffer books are distributed by
Bushwood Books
6 Marksbury Rd.
Kew Gardens
Surrey TW9 4JF England
Phone: 44 (0)181 392-8585; Fax: 44 (0)181 392-9876
E-mail: Bushwd@aol.com

Please try your bookstore first.

We are interested in hearing from authors with book ideas on related subjects.

Contents

Acknowledgements

This book could not have been written without the generous help and support of many collectors and dealers. We have never paid much attention to the acknowledgment sections of collector's books and price guides in the past. The experience of working on this book project has certainly changed that! So many people have generously shared their information, time, and glassware with us. Every contribution, large or small, has been vital in the process of putting this book together.

Some people warmly welcomed us in to their homes and gave us unlimited access to their collections. Others took the time to call and let us know about jadite they found. Was it rare? Did we need it for the book? Should they buy it for us? When time or geography made it difficult or impossible to schedule a photo shoot at their location, we were able to convince a few collectors to take photographs or ship their treasured glass to us.

Thanks go to Jane and Jerry Bohlen, Dennis English, and Anna and Joe Thomas for sharing their glass and allowing us to turn their homes in to photo studios. A very special thank you is due Dixie Hardesty. Dixie spent countless hours putting us in touch with collectors, tracking down rare or impossible to locate jadite, and helping to organize the photo shoots in Lancaster Ohio with Molly J. Allen, Jane and Jerry Bohlen, and Theresa and John Mitchell. In addition to the people previously mentioned, we would like to thank three very trusting collectors who loaned us the bulk of their collections for photo shoots: Cookie Katz, "who was jadite when jadite wasn't cool"; Joseph Keller, Sr., "who would pay up to one dollar for a piece of jadite when he collected!"; and Dalen Whitt, who trusted us with his great canister collection.

We are also grateful to Bill Granger, Sandy and Ron Levine, Shirley Moore, and Beckye Richardson for helping with the photography and/or loan of items from their collections. Special thanks to Scott Differ for his generous support of our efforts and for making our lives easier and happier during this green period.

The help and cooperation of Barb Wolff and her staff at Anchor Hocking was invaluable. Being allowed to sort through the shelves of old glass in the morgue at Anchor Hocking was fun and informative. We were able to photograph numerous prototypes and catalogues that greatly enriched our book. Knowing how many requests Barb receives for information related to Fire-king, we are very appreciative that she could fit us in to her busy schedule.

Thanks go to the staff of Schiffer Publishing for all their help with our first venture in to the wonderful world of publishing. Douglas Congdon-Martin helped keep the craziness at photo shoots under control and guide us in the right direction. Blair Loughrey kept the atmosphere relaxed and made the sometimes challenging photo shoots run smoothly. We are also grateful for Jeff Snyder's help.

The following people also gave of their time or collections to assist us with our book and we will be forever grateful for their contributions: Donna Berger, Steve Cacciola, Jerry & Kathy English, Ruthie & Winfield Foley, Phyllis & Shelley Galinken, Randy Hardesty, Shane Hardesty, Mike Kury, Dottie Milanoski, Norma Nye, Valerie Paknik, Stephen Rotondaro, Sue Springer, Betty Steen, Brad Waterman, and Suzanne Weatherman.

We have tried our best to mention all those that helped with what at times was an overwhelming project, but if any names were forgotten it was not from lack of appreciation. Thank you!

Pricing

Identifying values for jadite has been especially difficult due to the volatility of the market. The recent jadite craze, identified by dealers throughout the country, has obviously caused the values of these items to soar. The number of collectors wanting the same pieces at the same time has had the effect of dramatically inflating prices over the past 18 months. Antique dealers selling this merchandise have seen unprecedented requests for jadite. Prices have doubled and tripled on many of the most common pieces in a very short time. Most dealers remember a time not too long ago where most of the common jadite, especially Jane Ray dinnerware and Swirl mixing bowls, were difficult to sell. This has changed!

Another problem with jadite prices has been the fact that most pieces have been greatly undervalued in the more general Kitchenware and Fire-king price guides. Rare pieces of jadite have been consistently selling for many times "book value" for years. Ultimately supply and demand establish prices for any item. Yet with scarce items, the demand has been so high and supply so low, that it is perplexing that these items have been so undervalued for so long.

To establish prices, we have contacted leading dealers and collectors of kitchen glassware throughout the country. We have also watched and recorded prices in national publications like *The Daze* and *Antique Trader*, and on-line auctions like ebay™. We have not taken the highest or lowest price, nor a strict average. In many cases, we only have one or two sources to draw upon for the value of an item. The prices established in this book, however, are ultimately values that we have assigned based on this information and the trends as we see them.

Foreword

The popularity of jadite kitchenware and dinnerware in the past couple of years has grown to such an extent that we felt a book was needed that specifically focused on this collectible. While jadite has long been a supplemental part of many Depression Era Kitchen and glass books, no books specifically focused on this area. Our goal in creating this book is to bring together source information from many of these books and supply current values for a collectible that has defied trends in becoming so popular. While the focus of this book will be jadite, we have included items in other shades of green as well as occasionally in other colors, such as delfite and custard, if they provide information on jadite pieces that we have been unable to locate.

It has been difficult to define the parameters of this book. Jadite as a category of collectible is defined differently by many collectors. Most would agree that it includes the mass-produced, opaque green glassware made by McKee, Jeannette, and Anchor Hocking from the early 1930s to the mid 1970s. Yet many other companies produced household glassware that, in both color and form, should be included in this category.

We have decided to include as Jadite any opaque household glassware that is light green in color. We have decided to focus on the works of the three major companies and any items that closely resemble this glassware. Therefore we have included works by Morgantown, Fenton, Westmoreland, and others, but with these companies, we are much less comprehensive than we have attempted to be with Jeannette, McKee, and Anchor Hocking.

With the popularity of this glassware in recent years, the term "jadite" has frequently been extended to include anything green that resembles the color of jade. Similarly, any kitchenware made of glass without regard to its color has been referred to as jadite. Terms like "yellow jadite" and "jadite kitchen scale" have been adopted by many enthusiasts to extend the popularity, indeed the craze of jadite, to other related collectibles. We have included some of these related items to give the reader a sense of what is available in the marketplace.

Introduction

McKee Glass Company

The origins of jadite as a force in the glassware industry can be traced to its development by the McKee Glass Co. in 1930. While some jadite items were produced by other glass companies prior to this date, McKee's introduction of Skokie green and Jade kitchenware and dinnerware marks the first large-scale attempt to introduce jadite.

The McKee company was founded in 1853 as McKee and Brothers Glass Works. Originally located in Pittsburgh, the large company moved east to Westmoreland County in 1888 for economic and tax reasons. The town which the company founded, Jeannette Pa., was named for Mrs. Jeannette McKee. It would become a center of glass production for numerous glass companies over the following century.

McKee Tom and Jerry punch set.

A series of mergers and reorganizations in the early part of the 20th century resulted in a large company that produced both low-cost industrial glassware and handmade artistic lines. A series of patents and licenses to use other glass companies' techniques in the late teens and twenties enabled the company to move towards semi-automatic and eventually fully machine-made productions.[1] This made possible the mass-produced lines that would be necessary as the Depression affected the company's clientele. By the 1920s, McKee Glass Co. was producing a variety of household and industrial glassware, including lenses for most automobile headlights. McKee's ovenware line, *Glassbake*, rapidly became one of the most popular glassware lines in history and was produced for more than forty years.

The introduction of "opal wares" in the late 1920s and "jade glass" around 1930 by McKee marks the real beginnings of Jadite. According to company literature, opaque glassware was introduced in a variety of colors that were inspired by the various shades of opal and jade stones.[2] Included in these colors were French Ivory, Seville yellow, Poudre blue (also called "chaline" in company literature), opal white, and Skokie green. McKee's only complete line of Jadite dinnerware, Laurel, was introduced at this time. Laurel was most heavily marketed in French Ivory and Jadite, with fewer pieces being made in the poudre blue. Also introduced in 1930 and 1931 was a line of opaque kitchenware. This

McKee "Art Deco Nude" vases in chaline, dark jadite, and light jadite.

line included mixing bowls, shakers, canisters, refrigerator dishes, and orange juice reamers.

The mass-produced opaque lines were critical to the survival of the company. As Hazel Marie Weatherman in her *Colored Glassware of the Depression Era, Book 2* assesses, the unique opaque lines which include dinnerware, children sets, kitchenware, and even the Sunkist reamer helped maintain the company through a long difficult economic time.[3] Most of these items were made into the 1940s, but it is especially difficult to determine when individual items went out of production. Many of the company's metal molds were sold to the government in response to needs arising during World War II.[4] Other molds stayed active and were used throughout the life of the company.

McKee Glass Company was acquired by Thatcher Glass Manufacturing Company in 1951. Thatcher Glass was subsequently sold to the Jeannette Glass Company, whose operation then moved to the old McKee plant.

McKee jadite, for the most part, is marked with the letters "McK" in a small circle.

Jeannette Glass Company

Shortly after McKee's introduction of colored opaque kitchenware, its rival company in Jeannette, Pa.—the Jeannette Glass Company—began production of a similar line in 1932.

Founded in 1898 as a bottle producer, Jeannette Glass Company became a force in glass production in the 1920s with its advanced technology in the automation of colored glassware production. Contemporary trade journals refer to Jeannette as the first company to fully automate the production of pink and green glassware.[5] This enabled them to lower prices on mass-produced glassware and respond to the needs of the Depression era consumer.

Jeannette jadite kitchenware.

Jeannette's production of opaque kitchenware was clearly a response to McKee's successful line. Like McKee, Jeanette's product line included canisters, shakers, leftovers, and mixing bowls, available in a variety of colors. Jeannette's opaque green line was, for the first time, called "Jadite." Other companies would borrow this name, changing it to "Jad-ite" or "Jade-ite" over the following twenty years. Jeannette also produced a successful line of blue kitchenware, introduced in 1936 as "delfite."

Jeannette delfite kitchenware.

Jeannette produced no jadite dinnerware lines, yet continued to produce jadite kitchenware into the 1940s. In the 1950s, they acquired Thatcher Glass, who possessed many of the original McKee molds. Jeannette then produced many McKee items, including the Glassbake line and special orders, until the plant closed in the 1970s.

Most Jeannette jadite is not marked. Some of the earlier pieces are marked with a "J" in a triangle, followed by mold numbers.

Pages from 1952 Fire-king catalogue.

Anchor Hocking

Despite McKee's success with their Laurel line, it was more than a decade before another jadite dinnerware line was introduced. The vast majority of jadite dinnerware was made from 1945 to 1975 by Anchor Hocking under their Fire-king division.

Anchor Hocking Glass Corporation was created by the merger of Anchor Cap and Closure Corporation and the Hocking Glass Company in 1937. The company focused on the creation of mass-produced, inexpensive tableware and glass containers.

In the tradition of Hocking Glass, color played a major role in many of Anchor Hocking's new product lines. In 1939, they introduced the first of their royal ruby lines. This was followed in 1940 by "Philbe" dinnerware which was produced in pink, blue, and green. Philbe dinnerware was followed by ovenware with the Philbe design on it in 1942. This was marketed as "Fire-king" ovenware.

In the mid-1940s, Fire-king introduced dinnerware lines including, Alice, Jane Ray, and Restaurant Ware, that were available in several colors including jadite. Jane Ray and Restaurant Ware were complete lines; one being introduced for retail consumption, the other for commercial uses. Both were very successful and stayed in production for twenty years.

In the late 1940s and 1950s, many kitchen and household items were made in jadite by the Fire-king division of Anchor Hocking, including vases, refrigerator dishes, pitchers, and mixing bowls.

Most Fire-king jadite is marked with some variety of the company's Fire-king logo. Some pieces that were special orders for specific stores or promotions have no company marking.

Cover of 1955 catalogue depicting the Anchor Hocking factory.

[1]Sandra McPhee Stout, *The Complete Book of McKee Glass* (North Kansas City: Trojan Press, 1972), 16-18.
[2]Stout, 22.
[3]Hazel Marie Weatherman, *Colored Glassware of the Depression Era, Book II* (Springfield, MO.: Weatherman Glassbooks, 1974), 263.
[4]Stout, 21.
[5]*China, Glass, and Lamps* (Nov., 1928).

Fire-king jadite
ball jugs.

Magazine advertisement for Anchor Glass.

Record album. "Always" by the Anchorettes.

Kitchenware

Canisters

Canister sets were extremely popular during the Depression Era. Hoosier cabinets filled with cooking and baking utensils were a part of everyday life. While crystal and colored canisters were made by many glass companies during the 1920s and 1930s, McKee and Jeannette Glass Companies responded to the demand by producing more than a dozen styles of jadite canisters between 1931 and 1938. The typical canister set consisted of four canisters: coffee, tea, sugar, and either flour or cereal. In most styles of canister sets, at least five different canisters can usually be found.

McKee was first to produce jadite canisters. The earliest were the elusive column canisters and the square press-on lid canisters. These are very rarely found in today's marketplace and are highly prized by collectors. They were replaced by square canisters with screw-on lids, which were marketed as "2 piece" and "4 piece utility jar sets." The two-piece set consisted of coffee and tea, and therefore explains the relative scarcity of sugar, flour, and cereal canisters in this style.

McKee's round canisters with glass lids are found in at least three different heights and have three different styles of black lettering. They are found with jadite, black, and crystal round glass covers. The coffee canister, with script writing and a crystal cover, seems to be the most frequently found. Perhaps it was some type of promotional item.

McKee 48-ounce square cereal canister, press-on lid. $350–400.

McKee 48-ounce square canisters, press-on lid, 7 1/2".
Sugar, coffee, and tea canisters. Very Scarce. $350–400 each.

Jeannette made two square canister sets and one round. The square 48-ounce canisters and the round 40-ounce canisters can be found in both light and dark jadite. The dark tends to be the more difficult to locate. We have not found company literature that documents these two distinctly different shades.

The square 48-ounce canisters have Jeannette's Floral pattern impressed on the underside of the lids. These canisters are relatively common, but difficult to find with lids in good condition. The handles are too small to use and the overall size of the cover is too large to easily grasp. Jeannette's round canisters are only found in coffee, sugar, and tea, although numerous accessory pieces were made to compliment this set including, shakers, a refrigerator jar, and a vase.

The small 3" spice canisters were sold as a four-piece set with allspice, pepper, nutmeg, and ginger. A clove spice canister was also made, but is considerably more scarce. The children's canisters are sugar, flour, cereal, tea, and cocoa. We have heard reports of a coffee children's canister but have not seen it. All of the children's canisters are rare.

Collectors should be aware that most canisters can be found with or without lettering. All values in this book assume the item has vintage lettering. Items with new lettering do turn up in the marketplace and collectors should be aware of the difference. The round McKee tea canisters are an example of new and vintage lettering.

Jeannette column or vertical ribbed canister, with space for paper label, $350–400. We have not received any reports of a matching large size Jeannette canister.

Left: McKee Column canisters. These are the most rare of all canisters. Coffee, sugar, flour canisters, $800–1000 each. Tea canister, $500–700.

Below: McKee 48-ounce square canisters with screw-on lids, 7 1/4". Flour, cereal, tea, coffee, and sugar, $300–325 each.

McKee 28-ounce canisters. Tea, sugar, coffee, cereal. $250–275 each.

McKee 28-ounce flour canister and 48-ounce canister, 6 1/4". The 28-ounce flour canister is considered rare. $350–375.

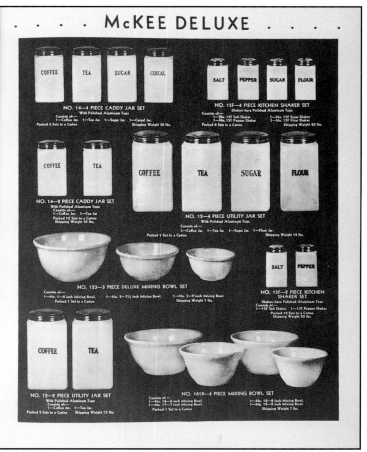

Page from McKee catalogue illustrating canisters and other kitchenware.

McKee round 48-ounce canisters with glass lids. Cereal, sugar, coffee, and tea. These are the largest of the McKee round canisters. $175–200 each

McKee round 40-ounce canisters with glass lids. Sugar, coffee, flour, and cereal. We have seen several of the 40-ounce sugar canisters and all are slightly shorter than the other canisters. $150–175.

McKee 40-ounce canisters with glass lids. Script lettering. Coffee canister $125-150, sugar and flour canisters $225–250 each.

Comparison of the three sizes of sugar canisters (left to right): 4 1/2", 5", 5 1/2".

13

Coffee canisters with jadite and crystal lids.

Comparison of tea canisters. The smaller tea canister has new lettering.

Jeannette 48-ounce Floral covered canister set. The Flour canister is considerably more scarce than the other four canisters. Cereal, tea, sugar, coffee canisters. $175–185 each. Flour canister $275–300. Prices are for canisters with lids in perfect condition.

Jeannette 29-ounce square canisters. Lids are the same as those found on the 4" x 4" refrigerator jar. Coffee, sugar, cereal, and tea canisters. We have had no reports of a flour canister in this size. $175–200 each.

Comparison of Jeannette square coffee canisters. Dark canisters are more difficult to find than light canisters. Add $25 for dark canisters.

Jeannette canister without lettering. $80–90.

Jeannette salt canister.
Extremely rare. $800–1000.

15

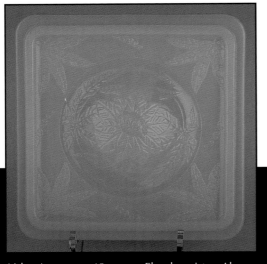

Lid to Jeannette 48-ounce Floral canister. Also fits the Jeannettte 5" x 5" refrigerator dish.

Comparison of light and dark 3" pepper canisters.

Jeannette 3" spice set: nutmeg, pepper, cloves, allspice, and ginger. The cloves cannister was not included in the standard set of four. Nutmeg $150–$175, pepper $125–150, cloves $400–500, allspice $150–175, ginger $150–175.

Jeannette 3" children's canisters. Rare. Flour, sugar, cocoa, and cereal. $500–600 each. Tea canister (not pictured) $500–600.

Jeannette round 40-ounce sugar canister, 40-ounce coffee canister, and 16-ounce tea canister in light Jadite. Sugar canisters are considerably more difficult to find than coffee or tea. Sugar $325–350, Coffee $225–250, Tea $150–175.

Jeannette 16-ounce tea canister, 40-ounce sugar canister, and 40-ounce coffee canister in dark jadite. Tea $200–225, sugar $350–375, coffee $250–275.

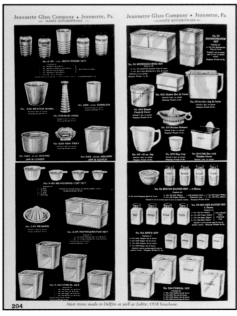

Pages from 1938 Jeannette brochure. From *Colored Glassware of the Depression Era, Book II,* by Hazel Marie Weatherman.

Comparison of light and dark sugar canisters.

Jeanette 40-ounce coffee canister and 16-ounce tea canister with painted strawberries. Many of the Jeannette pieces can be found with painted flowers or fruit. Most often found with a small painted flower, these items were most likely painted outside of the factory. Enough pieces have been found, with nearly identical painting, to indicate that these items were painted and marketed professionally. Painted pieces with the paint in good condition sell at a slight premium, normally 10–15% higher than undecorated examples.

Jeannette salt box with wooden cover. This is a large, heavy piece of Jadite. Scarce. $375–425.

Above: McKee salt box with metal lid. Made from the small mixing bowl. Uncommon piece. $175–200.

Right: 1931 advertisement of McKee kitchenware including salt box with metal lid. We had thought before that this piece was a sugar bowl with metal lid. From *Colored Glassware of the Depression Era, Book II*, by Hazel Marie Weatherman.

18

Jadite sugar bowl or salt box with metal cover. Unknown maker. $100–125.

Hocking canisters with paper labels. These are commonly found in green depression glass. Watch for internal cracks under the knob. New paper labels can be found for these canisters. $75–85 each.

Hazel Atlas fired-on green canister set. Complete and in excellent condition, $200–250.

Jeannette 29-ounce canister with hand-painted seagull scene. $125–150.

McKee roman arch sugar canister in white. None have been found in Jadite.

Mixing Bowls

Mixing bowls remain among the most popular of jadite pieces. Most everyone's grandmother or mother had at least one jadite mixing bowl in her kitchen. The bowls were well used and collectors frequently reminisce about a favorite food that was either prepared or served in them.

The McKee three-bowl round set was the earliest set produced. The smallest of these bowls doubled as a salt box with the addition of a metal cover. This set is quite scarce. More frequently found are the McKee bell-shaped bowls.

The Jeannette Glass Company also produced a three-bowl and four-bowl set. The three-bowl set consists of concentric ringed bowls and comes in both light and dark jadite. This set remains very popular with collectors as it contains the largest of all jadite mixing bowls. The four-bowl set is made up of vertical ribbed bowls and is only found in the lighter shade of jadite.

The Anchor Hocking Company produced five different styles of Fire-king mixing bowl sets. These were marketed as three- or four-bowl sets. In three of the five sets, an additional rare size bowl exists. The smallest of the splash proof and swirl sets are rare. The largest of the beaded-edge bowls is extremely rare.

The Colonial Kitchen and Swedish Modern sets are not commonly found. The smallest of the Swedish Modern is found much more frequently than the rest of the set. It may have been sold separately or as part of some promotion.

Splash Proof bowls with floral decals are scarce and highly sought-after by collectors. Prices on these bowls have skyrocketed recently. We have reports of several of these bowls selling for over $500 each.

McKee round mixing bowls. Scarce. 6" bowl $75–85, 7 1/2" bowl $80–90, 9" bowl $100–110.

McKee bell-shaped bowls. 6" bowl $30–35, 7" bowl $30–35, 8" bowl $35–40, 9" bowl $50–60.

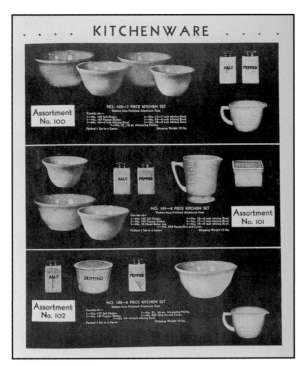

McKee catalogue depicting mixing bowls and other kitchenware.

Jeannette mixing bowls with concentric rings. Light color. 5 1/2" bowl $80–90, 7 1/2" bowl $100–110, 9 3/4" bowl $125–150.

Comparison of light and dark McKee 7 1/2" bowls. Prices for dark bowls are $10–20 higher than light bowls.

Splash proof mixing bowls. The one-quart size is especially rare. One qt. 6 3/4" $450–500, two qt. 7 1/2" $65–75, three qt. 8 1/2" $100–125, four qt. 9 1/2" $100–125.

Jeannette vertical ribbed mixing bowls. 6" bowl $25–30, 7" bowl $25–30, 8" bowl $30–35, 9" bowl $75–100.

Swirl mixing bowls with original cardboard dividers.

Swirl mixing bowls. The four bowl set is quite common. The smallest bowl measures 5" across and is quite scarce. 5" bowl $175–200, 6" bowl $20–25, 7" bowl $20–25, 8" bowl $25–30, 9" bowl $30–35.

Beaded Edge mixing bowls. The largest size is rare in jadite. 4 7/8" bowl $25–30, 6" bowl $20–25, 7" bowl $30–35, 8 3/8" bowl $450–500.

Colonial Mixing Bowls. 6" bowl $120–130, 7 1/4"
bowl $100–110, 8 3/4" bowl $100–125.

Above: Swedish Modern mixing bowls. Measurements indicate the
width not the length of the bowls. Complete set of four $600–650.
The smallest bowl is much more common than all other sizes. 5"
one pt. bowl $65–75, 6" one qt. bowl $200–225, 7 1/4" 2 qt. bowl
$150–175, 8 3/8" 3 qt. bowl $150–175.

Right: Swedish Modern
mixing bowl label. Adds
$50–75 to the value of
bowl.

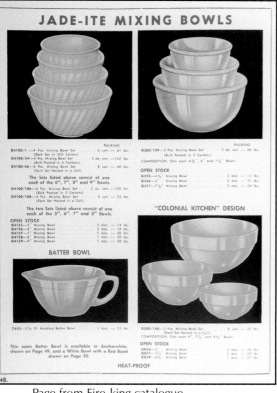

Page from Fire-king catalogue
advertising mixing bowls.

Above: Fire-king mixing bowl sets.

Left: Rare splash proof mixing bowls with red and white floral decorations. The 1-quart is more frequently found with decorations than plain. $400–600 each.

Below: Splash proof bowls with white decorations. $450–650 each.

Fire-king ribbed bowls. The 4 3/4" bowl is the most scarce of the three. The 4 3/4" bowl and 5 1/2" bowl can be found with lids as refrigerator dishes. 4 3/4" bowl $100–125, 5 1/2" bowl $40–45, 7 1/2" bowl $50–60. We have heard no reports of the 6" bowl existing in jadite, although it does exist in crystal and forest green.

Anchor Hocking clambroth mixing bowls with black trim. They can also be found without black trim. 5 1/2", 6 1/2" and 8" across. $175–200 set.

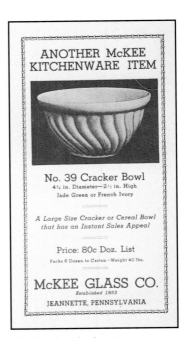

Cracker bowl advertisement.

McKee large serving bowl. This bowl is the same size as the Tom and Jerry punch bowl. $75–100.

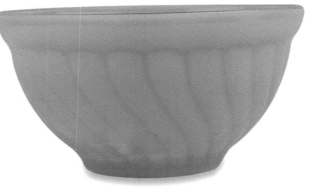

McKee bowl. 4 3/4" in diameter, 2 1/2" high. Advertised by McKee as "No 39 Cracker Bowl...A large size cracker or cereal bowl." $50–60.

Ovenware and Cookware

Each of the three major companies produced a limited line of items used for baking and cooking. McKee's contribution was limited to oval bakers, custards, and rolling pins. The bakers and custards are found plain and with a floral decorated border. The rolling pins are elusive and an impressive addition to any jadite collection. Both styles of rolling pins are hollow with one handle capped with a shaker lid. The pins could be filled with ice chips or ice water to keep dough chilled. The shaker lid would also make it possible to sprinkle the dough with water when necessary.

Jeannette's four-piece measuring cup set can be found with a decorated box that depicts a woman using Jeannette products. Decorated boxes were used very rarely when marketing mass-produced products during this era. The only other commonly found decorated jadite box is for the Jane Ray starter set.

Most of the Fire-king ovenware pieces are extremely rare. Only the saucepans and the plain custard are regularly found. The two covered casseroles never went into regular production, and thus are the holy grail for Fire-king collectors. Only a few have been found. The small handled french casserole occasionally turns up in the Ohio area, but they are also quite scarce. The Philbe pie plates tend to be more expensive than rare.

Fire-king legend has it that Hazel Marie Weatherman, the pioneer researcher of Depression and kitchen glassware, named the Philbe design. Mrs. Weatherman had a habit of naming items that she could not find referenced and named in company literature. When researching Fire-king, she located the man who created this design and found out that it did not have a name. The designer's son, Philip B., was present at this conversation and Mrs. Weatherman decided to name the design "Philbe" after him.

McKee oval baking dishes. Plain or decorated. $50–60 each.

McKee plain custard next to oval baking dish. Plain custard $20–25.

McKee custard with decoration. $35–40.

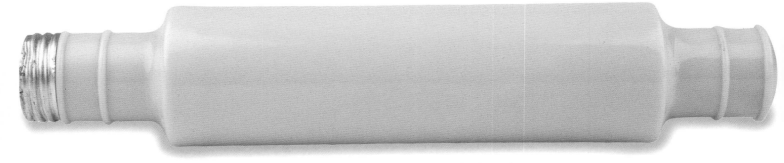

McKee rolling pin with metal screw-on lid. This is the more common of the two jadite rolling pins, $800–850.

Side view of the jadite rolling pin showing the screw-on shaker top.

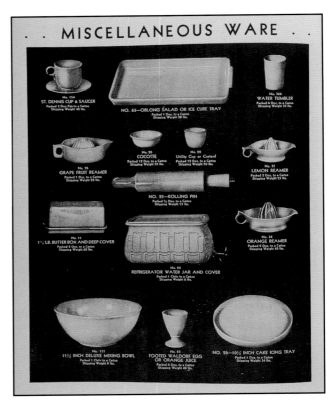

Page from McKee catalogue advertising jadite rolling pin and other kitchenware pieces. This ad depicts three items that we have not been able to locate—the two trays and the cup and saucer.

McKee rolling pin with metal screw-on lid. $900–950.

Jeannette measuring cups in original box. An interesting difference exists between the jadite and delphite sets. The jadite one-cup has a smooth edge; the delphite has a pouring spout. One-cup $50–60, 1/2 cup $45–50, 1/3 cup $40–45, 1/4 cup $30–35. Original box in good condition, $50–60. Complete set in box, $225–250.

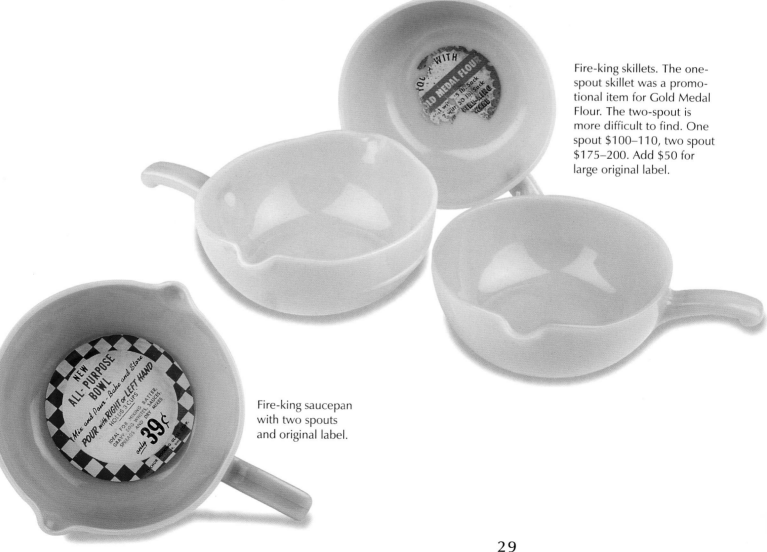

Fire-king skillets. The one-spout skillet was a promotional item for Gold Medal Flour. The two-spout is more difficult to find. One spout $100–110, two spout $175–200. Add $50 for large original label.

Fire-king saucepan with two spouts and original label.

Custard and bean pot. This bean pot is jadite, not fired-on green. From left: Fire-king 6-ounce custard, $90–100. Small 3″ bean pot from the morgue, dated 1952, $500+.

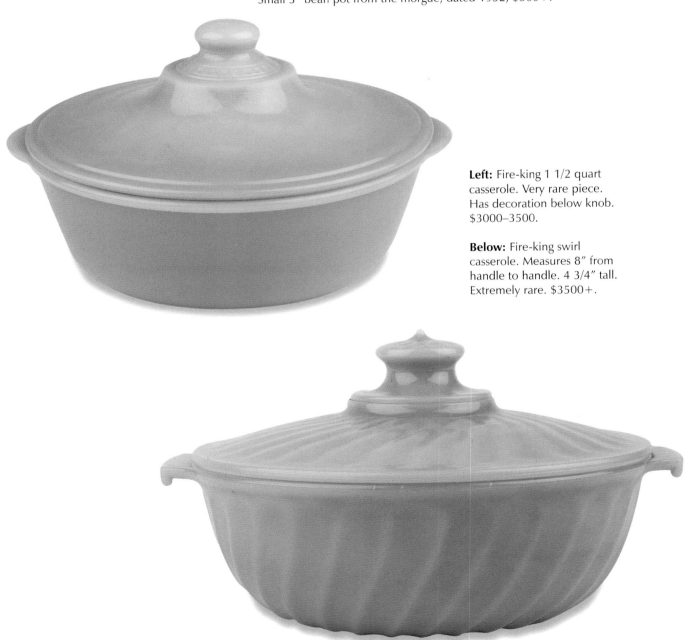

Left: Fire-king 1 1/2 quart casserole. Very rare piece. Has decoration below knob. $3000–3500.

Below: Fire-king swirl casserole. Measures 8″ from handle to handle. 4 3/4″ tall. Extremely rare. $3500+.

Small handled casserole/custards. 5" french casserole with crystal cover, $450–500. 4 5/16" handled casserole/custard, $600–750.

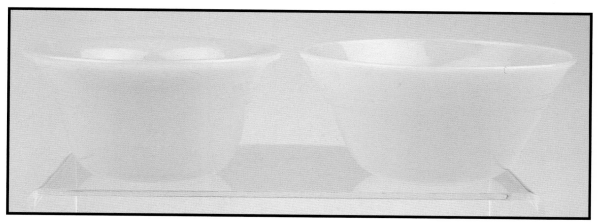

Two rare Philbe custards. Left: Flared custard 3 3/4" across top. Right: Straight-sided 4 1/16" across. $250–350 each.

Fire-king ovenware label.
Adds $25 to value of item.

Close-up of Philbe design on custard.

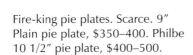

Fire-king pie plates. Scarce. 9"
Plain pie plate, $350–400. Philbe
10 1/2" pie plate, $400–500.

Underside of Philbe pie plate.

Decorated label for Philbe pie
plates. Adds $50 to value of item.

Fire-king custards from the
morgue. From left: 5" Small
flanged bowl, 3 5/8" ribbed
custard, 3 5/8" plain custard.
$400–500 each.

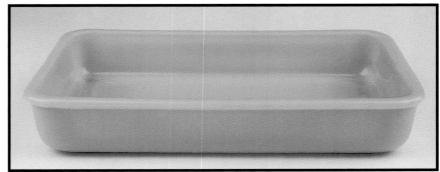

McKee baking dish.
Rare. 8 1/4" x 12 3/4".
$250–275.

Reamers

Orange juice reamers could be found in most Depression era kitchens. The increased availability of citrus products made fresh juice at home possible. Reamers were marketed and given away as promotions by citrus companies, like Sunkist, to help sell their product.

McKee and Jeannette each made a variety of styles of reamers for oranges, lemons, and grapefruit. McKee also made jadite attachments for electrical appliances that made juice. See the Kitchen Appliance section.

The Sunkist reamer by McKee was made in several different shades of jadite, as well as in a large variety of colors, including blue, black, green and yellow. It is most frequently seen in white.

Jadite reamers. Clockwise from left: McKee lemon, $45–50. Jeannette orange, $50–60. Jeannette lemon, $45–50. McKee orange, $50–60. McKee Sunkist, $50–60.

Jeannette Measuring pitcher with reamer top. Found in both light and dark Jadite. Measuring pitcher holds two cups. The base of pitcher has a sunflower design. The reamer top also was marketed separately. Light pitcher with reamer top, $125–135. Dark pitcher with reamer top, $140–150. Reamer top alone, $30–35.

McKee Grapefruit Reamer. Difficult to find with reamer ribs in good condition. $150–175.

Refrigerator Dishes and Butter Dishes

Jadite storage dishes are among the most popular and practical of all jadite pieces. Most of these items were popular and reasonable in their day and thus easily found today. Most of the refrigerator dishes were sold in three-piece sets.

The crystal covered Fire-king 1/4-pound butter is the most plentiful of the butter dishes. It is also the butter dish most in demand. The larger butters are less practical in today's kitchen. They are also more difficult to find in good condition. The bases of the large butters are almost always damaged from use.

Drippings containers were used to keep animal fat on the stove for future use. The round Jeannette drippings container and the Fire-king grease jar are relatively easy to find, unlike the two square McKee drippings jars, which are extremely rare. A third McKee dripping can be seen in company literature at the end of this section, although we have had no reports of this piece. All of the drippings containers were also marketed without writing as refrigerator dishes.

A variety of large refrigerator pans were made in both jadite and clambroth. These are frequently found with the name of the refrigerator company embossed on the side or base. These pans are not especially popular with collectors. They are extremely large and heavy, and while they are impressive pieces of glass, they serve little function today.

The ribbed Fire-king butter and refrigerator dish are extremely rare. We only know of one of each of these pieces. Both have solid crystal counterparts that are relatively common. Perhaps other Fire-king pieces that were made in great quantity in crystal will turn up in jadite.

Many refrigerator dishes have covers that were used on other items. The cover for the Jeannette square refrigerator dish also fits the square 29-ounce canister. The crystal covers for Fire-king pieces were used on other color bases as well. Collectors frequently match covers from less expensive items with more expensive bases. Color and fit sometimes can be a problem. Most of these pieces were made for long periods of time and many different molds and color dye lots were used. It may take more than one try to make an adequate match.

Above: McKee leftovers. Sold as a three-piece set with matching lids. Lids were available in crystal or jadite. 4" x 5" with jadite cover, $25–30. 4" x 5" with crystal cover, $18–20. 5" x 8" with jadite cover, $40–45.

Right: McKee leftovers. 4" x 5", $35–40. 5" x 8", $60–65.

McKee 4" x 6" leftover with knob lid. Rare. $125–150.

Clambroth leftover with crystal cover. $25–30.

Above: McKee refrigerator dishes. Scarce. Available in two sizes, 6 1/4" and 7". These refrigerator storage boxes were available with or without the McKee embossed floral design. We have found both handled and handless bases. The bottom of one of these is marked "Glassbake". Tops are marked "This side up." Small size $125–150, large size $150–175.

Right: Close-up on McKee floral design.

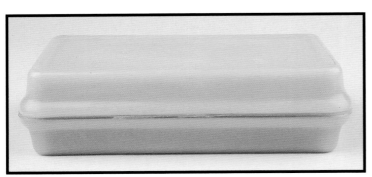

McKee cheese dish. At first glance, this piece appears to be two butter bottoms put together, but actually there is a distinct top and bottom to this piece. Very unusual. $200–250.

Jeannette leftover sets. 4" x 4" $25–30, 4" x 8" $40–45, 5" x 5" with Floral lid $65–75, 5"x10" $65–75.

McKee 6-piece refrigerator set. These jars were sold individually and as a set. The large size was sold with lettering as canisters. Company literature shows the middle size with "drippings" in black letters. Small jar with cover $30–35, medium jar $50–60, large jar $75–85.

Jeannette round crocks/ leftovers. 4 1/4" high x 6" wide, $100–110. 3 1/2" high x 6" wide, $50–60.

Above: The fire-king loaf pan measures 5″ x 9″ and is exactly the same as the base to the Philbe rectangular refrigerator dish except it does not have the Philbe design. Loaf pan, $75–100. Philbe covered refrigerator dish, $50–60.

Right: Close-up of Philbe design on cover of 5″ x 9″ refrigerator dish.

Above: Clambroth oval leftover. $35–40.

Right: Philbe leftovers. 4 1/2″ x 5″. Can be found with plain and decorated bases. $30–35.

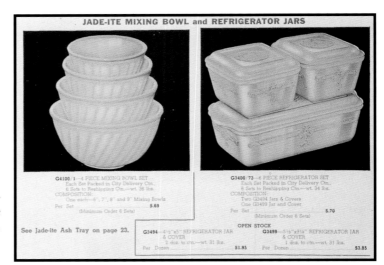

Catalogue advertisement for Philbe refrigerator dishes.

Crystal covered Fire-king jadite leftovers. 4" x 4", $25–30. 4" x 8", $45–50.

Catalogue advertisement for leftovers and butter dish.

Fire-king rectangular ribbed leftover with crystal cover from the morgue. 8 3/4" x 5". No backstamp. $350+.

Ribbed Fire-king bowl with crystal covers. 4 3/4" bowl with cover, $100–125. 5 1/2" bowl with cover, $40–45.

Clambroth leftovers with crystal lids. 4 1/4" x 5", $20–25. 4 1/8" x 6 1/4", $25–30. 3 5/8" x 3 5/8", $15–20.

Above: Triangular covered jar with Jadite cover. Large "S" on side. $75–85.

Right: Martha Stewart 1998 refrigerator dishes. Retailed at $44 for the pair. Made by Fenton. Marked on bottom "MBM" for Martha by Mail™.

Jeannette round leftover. Same as drippings without lettering. $30–35.

Drippings jars. Jeannette round drippings, $150–175. McKee square drippings, $300–400.

Above: McKee square drippings jars. Scarce. Left: Plain lid, $300–400. Right: Lid with raised internal border, $400–500.

Right: Fire-king grease jar. $60–70.

Above, right, and below:
"Stewart-Warner" refrigerator pan. 11 1/2" x 13 1/2". This is one of the most commonly seen of the refrigerator pans. It is signed on its side. $75–100.

Clambroth refrigerator pan.
2" high. 7" x 16". $65–75.

McKee butter dishes. One-pound and 1 1/4-pound. The smaller one-pound butter dish is considerably more scarce than the larger size. This piece is difficult to find without rim roughness on the base. Notice the ridges on the sides of the cover and the medallion on cover. One-pound butter, $200–250. 1 1/4-pound, $175–200.

Jeannette butter and cover with embossed "Butter" on cover. Collectors have come to accept some minor roughness on the base of this piece. It is almost impossible to find in mint condition. $150–175.

Clambroth tall butter dish. $150–175.

Fire-king butter dish. Crystal cover on jadite base. $100–125.

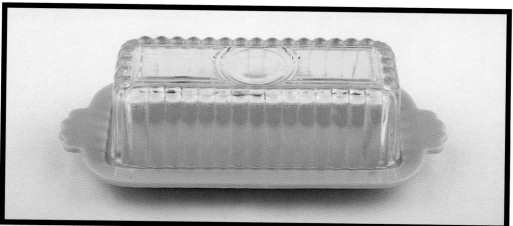

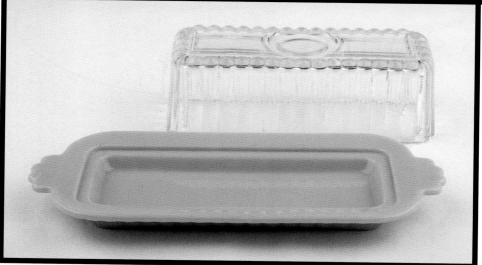

Fire-king ribbed butter with crystal cover. This piece is common with a crystal base, but is extremely rare with jadite base. $1500–2000.

Shakers

Like canisters, McKee and Jeannette each made several different styles of shakers. Most common in all lines are the salt and pepper shakers. Company literature indicates that these could be purchased as pairs or in sets with sugar and flour. Any shakers besides the basic four are scarce. We have not found any literature to indicate how these other shakers were marketed.

McKee made three styles of shakers: the square shakers with block print, the square shakers with letters in a black box, and the roman arch shakers. In addition to the four basic shakers, the square shakers with block print are pictured with ginger, nutmeg, and allspice. We have also seen photos of talcum and soap powder shakers. The shakers with letters in a box come in two different sizes of boxes, which we have called small box and large box. Eight different small box shakers are pictured. We have only located five of the large box, but would bet that all eight exist. The roman arch shakers are considerably more scarce than the other two styles. These are more frequently seen in black amethyst and white. Additionally McKee produced square shakers with flowers and vertical lines. Both of these sets are scarce.

Notice the two rare styles of McKee shakers: the salesman's sample shakers that have flowers on one side and vertical lines on the other, and the advertising shaker. The advertising shaker is for a beer company and lists a different product on each side.

Jeannette also produced three different styles of shakers: square, 6-ounce ribbed, and 8-ounce ribbed. All can be found in both light and dark jadite, although the 6-ounce shakers are especially scarce in the dark color. The 6-ounce shakers were made for "Big Hit" spices and frequently are found with some portion of their paper label still intact. They are considerably more scarce when found with black lettering. The 8-ounce ribbed salt and pepper are the most frequently found of all jadite shakers.

Notice the Jeannette delphite ginger. The lettering matches that of the McKee ginger and not that of other Jeannette pieces.

The only Fire-king shakers are the range shakers with metal cover that depict tulips. Finding these covers in good condition can be difficult.

McKee allspice shaker. Rare. $250–300.

McKee square shakers. Salt $35–40, pepper $35–40, flour $50–60, sugar $50–60, ginger $200–250, nutmeg $200–250.

McKee square small box shakers. Salt $40–45, pepper $40–45, sugar $60–65, flour $60–65, ginger $150–175, cinnamon $175–200, spice $175–200, nutmeg $150–175.

McKee sqare large box shakers. The spice shaker is extremely rare. Salt $50–60, pepper $50–60, spice $200–225, sugar $65–75, flour $65–75.

McKee custard large box shakers. We were unable to locate these items in jadite, but they should exist. In custard, $40–50 each. In jadite, $200+ each.

McKee roman arch shakers with large "S" and "P". Scarce. $75–100. each.

McKee roman arch cinnamon. Rare. $200–225. Nutmeg (not pictured) $200–250.

McKee Roman Arch shakers. Jadite shakers are scarce, especially spice and cinnamon. Salt $75–85, flour $100–125, sugar $100–125, pepper $75–85, spice $200–225.

McKee custard shakers with vertically printed letters in french. We have not located these shakers in jadite. In custard, $75–100 each

McKee square shakers with vertical lines and vertically printed letters. Rare. Salt $125–150, pepper $125–150, flour $200–225, sugar $200–225.

McKee square shakers with flowers. Scarce. Salt $100–125, pepper $100–125, sugar $125–150, flour $125–150.

McKee square salesman's sample shakers. Flowers on
one side, vertical lines on the other. Rare. $500+ pair.

Label on salesman's sample reads, "Sample
mfd. by The Tipp Tovcky Co., Tippecanoe
City, O." This company must have decorated and marketed some McKee shakers.

McKee flour shaker
with deco design.
Rare. $200–250.

McKee square shaker that has a different advertisement
for Huether's Beer on each side. $300–350.

Jeannette 6-ounce shakers with black lettering. Scarce. Salt $75–85, pepper $75–85, flour $90–100, sugar $90–100.

Jeannette 6-ounce spice shakers made for Big Hit spices. $30–35 each. Without labels $20–22.

Jeannette round 8-ounce shakers. Light color. Salt $35–40, pepper $35–40, sugar $65–75, flour $65–75.

Jeannette round 8-ounce shakers. Dark color. Salt $40–50, pepper $40–50, sugar $75–85, flour $75–85.

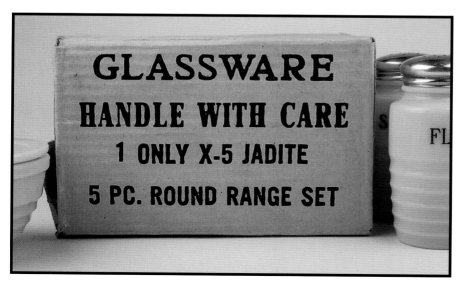

Above: Jeannette boxed set. Includes sugar, flour, salt, pepper shakers and a drippings jar with lid. Boxes in good condition are scarce and quite desirable. $375–400 set.

Left: Close-up on the side of box.

Jeannette decorated shakers and drippings jar. Salt $50–60, pepper $50–60, drippings jar $200–225.

Jeannette square range shakers. Dark color. Pepper $50–60, salt $50–60, sugar $75–85, flour $75–85.

Jeannette square range shakers. Light color. Salt $45–50, pepper $45–50, flour $65–75, sugar $65–75, allspice (rare) $225–250.

Jeannette delphite ginger and McKee jadite ginger. Notice the similarity in the lettering. Delphite ginger, $200+.

Jeannette 6-ounce and 8-ounce shakers with a variety of lettering, labels, and covers. The minced onion label is a decal of questionable vintage.

Jeannette sugar shakers with vertical ribs.
Dark Jadite $125–150, light jadite $100–125.

Jadite 5 1/4" ribbed shakers.
$100–125/pair.

Hocking clambroth shaker with paper label. $20–25 each.

Above: Fire-king shakers with tulip covers, $65–75 pair. Grease jar with tulip cover, $60–70.

Left: Page from Fire-king catalogue advertising range set.

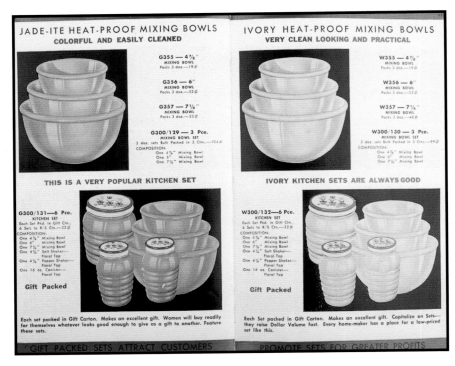

JADE-ITE HEAT-PROOF MIXING BOWLS
COLORFUL AND EASILY CLEANED

G355 — 4 7/8" MIXING BOWL Packs 3 doz.—19#

G356 — 6" MIXING BOWL Packs 3 doz.—32#

G357 — 7 1/4" MIXING BOWL Packs 3 doz.—53#

G300/129 — 3 Pce. MIXING BOWL SET
3 doz. sets Bulk Packed in 3 Ctns.—104#
COMPOSITION:
One 4 7/8" Mixing Bowl
One 6" Mixing Bowl
One 7 1/4" Mixing Bowl

THIS IS A VERY POPULAR KITCHEN SET

G300/131—6 Pce. KITCHEN SET
Each Set Pkd. in Gift Ctn.
6 Sets to R/S Ctn.—32#
COMPOSITION:
One 4 7/8" Mixing Bowl
One 6" Mixing Bowl
One 7 1/4" Mixing Bowl
One 4 1/4" Salt Shaker—Floral Top
One 4 1/4" Pepper Shaker—Floral Top
One 16 oz. Canister—Floral Top

Gift Packed

Each set packed in Gift Carton. Makes an excellent gift. Women will buy readily for themselves whatever looks good enough to give as a gift to another. Feature these sets.

GIFT PACKED SETS ATTRACT CUSTOMERS

IVORY HEAT-PROOF MIXING BOWLS
VERY CLEAN LOOKING AND PRACTICAL

W355 — 4 7/8" MIXING BOWL Packs 3 doz.—19#

W356 — 6" MIXING BOWL Packs 3 doz.—32#

W357 — 7 1/4" MIXING BOWL Packs 3 doz.—53#

W300/130 — 3 Pce. MIXING BOWL SET
3 doz. sets Bulk Packed in 3 Ctns.—99#
COMPOSITION:
One 4 7/8" Mixing Bowl
One 6" Mixing Bowl
One 7 1/4" Mixing Bowl

IVORY KITCHEN SETS ARE ALWAYS GOOD

W300/132—6 Pce. KITCHEN SET
Each Set Pkd. in Gift Ctn.
6 Sets to R/S Ctn.—32#
COMPOSITION:
One 4 7/8" Mixing Bowl
One 6" Mixing Bowl
One 7 1/4" Mixing Bowl
One 4 1/4" Salt Shaker—Floral Top
One 4 1/4" Pepper Shaker—Floral Top
One 16 oz. Canister—Floral Top

Gift Packed

Each Set packed in Gift Carton. Makes an excellent gift. Capitalize on Sets—they raise Dollar Volume fast. Every home-maker has a place for a low-priced set like this.

PROMOTE SETS FOR GREATER PROFITS

Fired-on green shakers with deco design. Flour $20–25, pepper $15–20, salt $15–20.

Laurel

Laurel has the distinction of being the earliest mass-produced jadite dinnerware and the only set not produced by Anchor Hocking. It was produced by McKee in 1931. In addition to jadite, it is also found in french ivory and poudre blue with the blue being especially scarce.

On some pieces, the leaf design can be especially weak. This can be best seen with the shakers. Finding shakers is difficult enough; finding them with a strong pattern design is almost impossible. Flat pieces were produced with plain and scalloped edges. The pieces with scalloped edges are prone to chips and all pieces in this line come with heavy mold roughness.

Not pictured are the Laurel 8" flat soup, the short footed candles, and the short sugar and creamer. The 4" wine goblet is exceptionally scarce. The leaves on the wine goblet are slightly different than those found on other pieces of Laurel, yet similar enough to be included with this pattern. A matching decanter has been reported.

The children's set was marketed plain and with Scottie dog decorations. Collectors in search of Scottie dog pieces are faced with heavy competition. It is sought after by Scottie dog, jadite, and children's dish collectors.

LAUREL PATTERN TABLEWARE
New French Ivory Glass Dinnerware

Above: Original Laurel advertisement. From *Colored Glassware of the Depression Era, Book II* by Hazel Marie Weatherman.

Left: Laurel bowls. Clockwise from left: 11" round utility bowl, $60–70. 9" round vegetable dish, $35–40. 9" oval vegetable dish, $45–50. "3 toe jelly" $30–35. 6" cereal dish with flanged rim, $20–22. 6" oatmeal (listed as 5" in company catalogues), Scarce, $35–40. In center: 5" fruit dish, $12–15. Not pictured: 8" flat soup (listed as 9" in company catalogue), $75–85.

Laurel plates. 9" dinner plate, $20–25. 7 1/2" salad plate which doubles as the base of the cheese dish, $20–25. 6" Plate, $10–12.

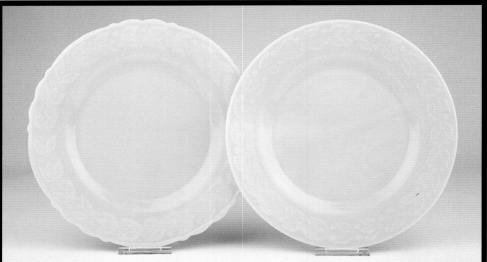

Two Laurel dinner plates, scalloped and plain edge. The scalloped seem to be more common. All sizes of plates, including the grill, can be found in both styles. No price difference.

Above: Laurel cup and saucer, $15–18.

Right: Laurel No 1. Tall sugar and creamer. This is the more frequently found of the two sugar and creamer sets, $45–50 set. Laurel No. 2 short sugar and creamer (not pictured), $50–60.

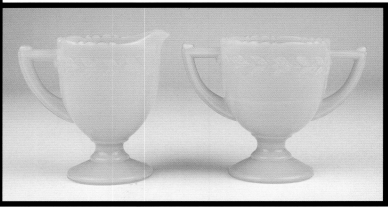

Laurel 9" grill plate, $25–30. Laurel 11" oval platter, $35–40.

Laurel wine goblet, scarce, $125–150. Laurel sherbet, $18–20.

Above: "3 toe jelly": a 6" bowl with three small knobs for feet. $30–35.

Left: Laurel salt and pepper. It is especially difficult to find shakers with a strong pattern. $75–100.

Laurel cheese dish. This is a favorite of collectors and has greatly increased in value over the past year. The base is the salad plate. $250–300.

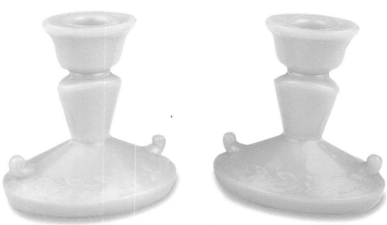

Laurel 4″ candlesticks. The blank for these candles was used for other McKee candlesticks with different designs. Design is frequently not strong on this piece. $75–85 pair.

McKee Laurel Dinnerware
French Ivory, Jade Green and White Opal

9″ DINNER PLATE   7½″ SALAD PLATE   6″ BREAD & BUTTER PLATE

OVAL VEGETABLE DISH   OVAL PLATTER   9″ ROUND VEGETABLE DISH

6″ 3 TOE JELLY   NO. 2 SUGAR BOWL   NO. 2 CREAMER   5″ OATMEAL

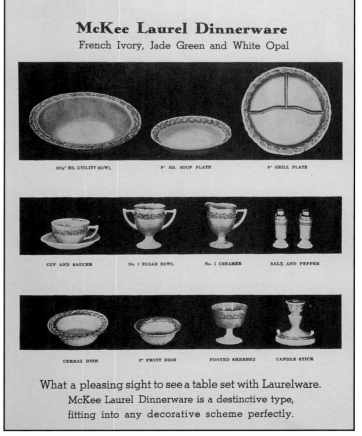

McKee Laurel Dinnerware
French Ivory, Jade Green and White Opal

10½″ RD. UTILITY BOWL   9″ RD. SOUP PLATE   9″ GRILL PLATE

CUP AND SAUCER   No. 1 SUGAR BOWL   No. 1 CREAMER   SALT AND PEPPER

CEREAL DISH   5″ FRUIT DISH   FOOTED SHERBET   CANDLE STICK

What a pleasing sight to see a table set with Laurelware. McKee Laurel Dinnerware is a destinctive type, fitting into any decorative scheme perfectly.

Catalogue advertisements for Laurel dinnerware

Laurel children's sugar bowls.

Laurel Hostess Tea Set for children. This set was made in green and ivory. It comes with and without Scottie dogs. The set consists of 4 cups, 4 saucers, 4 plates, 1 sugar, and 1 creamer. Round plates are more frequently found than scalloped plates.

	Jadite with Scottie Dog	Plain Jadite
Creamer	$125–150	$40–45
Cup	$90–100	$30–35
Plate	$50–60	$10–12
Saucer	$50–60	$12–15
Sugar	$125–150	$40–45
Complete	$1100–1200	$300–375

Alice dinnerware.

Alice

Alice was one of the earliest of Anchor Hocking's dinnerware lines. It was introduced in 1945, with only three pieces being produced: dinner plate, cup, and saucer. The cup and saucer were given away with the purchase of oatmeal and are very common. The dinner plate is considerably more scarce.

Alice was also produced in Anchor Hocking's vitrock, in both solid white and white with red or blue trim.

Alice cup and saucer, $10–12.

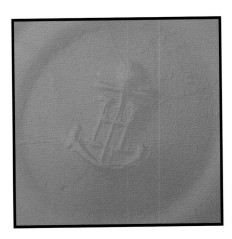

Anchor Hocking backstamp. Found on some Alice dinner plates.

Alice 9 1/4″ Dinner plate. Scarce. $35–40.

Banded

Very little of Anchor Hocking's "Banded" dinnerware was produced in jadite. "Banded" dinnerware really represents three different patterns: One Band, Two Bands, and Three Bands. We were able to photograph a few examples from the morgue at Anchor Hocking. The only pieces of banded we have owned are a One Band cup and a Three Bands vegetable bowl. In addition to the jadite pieces pictured, a Two Bands chili bowl, a Three Bands saucer, and a Three Bands dinner plate all have been found. We have had a report of a Three Bands dinner plate selling for $2000! Three Bands dinnerware is also found in ivory and maroon.

Above & left: Fire-king Three Bands 8" vegetable bowl with maroon 5" fruit bowl. Three band vegetable $125–150. The maroon fruit is from the morgue. NV

Three Band cup next to One Band cup and saucer. Three Band cup, $125–150.

One Band cup and saucer. Rare. $150–175.

Ivory Three Band dinner plate. $20–25.

61

Charm

Charm dinnerware was produced from the early to mid-1950s. Its distinctive square shape gave it a modern look that appealed to the post-war consumer. In addition to jadite, the charm shape was produced in azurite blue, forest green, and royal ruby.

Charm was marketed as a luncheon set which helps to explain the scarcity of many of the pieces. The lunch plate is the only easily found of the three plates. The practically sized 6" soup bowl and the large serving pieces are in short supply. The availability of jadite charm never seems to match the demand.

Charm Dinnerware.

Charm cup and saucer, $12–15.

Charm sugar and creamer. Sugar $20–25, creamer $20–25.

Charm plates. 6 5/8" Salad plate, $40–45. 8 3/8" lunch, $18–20. 9 1/4" dinner, $50–55.

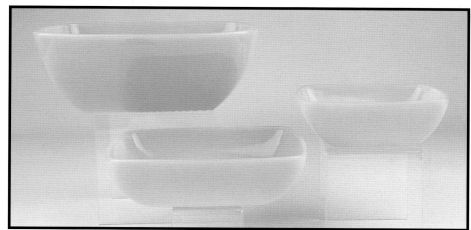

Charm bowls. 4 3/4" dessert $15–18, 6" soup $50–60, 7 3/8" salad bowl $65–75.

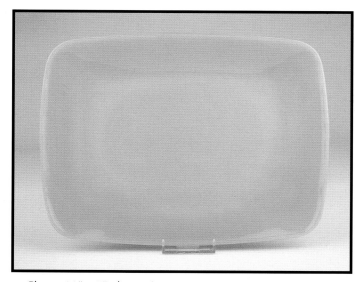

Charm 11" x 8" platter, $70–80.

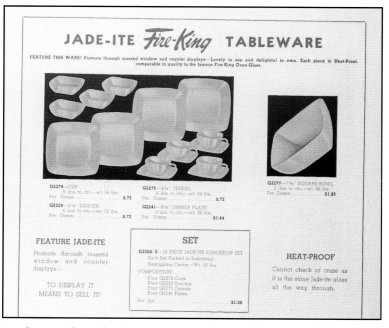

Fire-king catalogue brochure advertising Charm dinnerware.

Jane Ray

Jane Ray is the most common of the Fire-king dinnerware lines. Given its name by collectors more than a decade ago, this was one of the few Fire-king jadite lines that was extensively marketed for retail consumption. Jane Ray lacks the heaviness of some of Fire-king's other lines. Each piece is decorated with a rayed border and a plain center.

Until recently, Jane Ray was the dud of jadite dinnerware. Most dealers would carry only the better pieces in the line. Even now, the supply of Jane Ray cups and saucers seems like it will never dry up. The cups, saucers, and dinner plates were heavily marketed in give-away promotions and in starter sets. Thus, dinner plates are much more common than salad plates and all sizes of bowls.

There are some rare pieces in this line. The bread and butter plate is quite rare. It is slightly larger than the saucer. We have had several reports of collectors finding these in Canada. The flanged soup is also very difficult to locate. It has a distinct lip as opposed to the commonly found flat soup. The demitasse cup and saucer are scarce with the cup being more difficult to find than the saucer. (Unlike the restaurant demitasse cup and saucer, where the cup is relatively common and the saucer is scarce.)

Decorated boxes for starter sets are relatively common. This is one of the few decorated boxes for jadite that can be found. Larger sets were purchased in undecorated cardboard boxes.

This line has become quite popular with jadite's new enthusiasts. Unlike Fire-king Restaurant Ware, one can put together a complete dinner service without too much trouble or expense. The strong demand for basic pieces has dramatically affected prices which have more than doubled over the past eighteen months. We expect that this demand will continue until Jane Ray prices approach those of Restaurant Ware.

Jane Ray dinnerware.

Jane Ray plates. The 6 1/4" plate is extremely rare. 9 1/8" Dinner $12–14, 7 3/4" salad plate $12–15, 6 1/4" bread plate $150–175.

Jane Ray bowls. Clockwise from top: 8 1/4" Vegetable bowl $35–40, 7 5/8" soup plate $20–25, 5 7/8" cereal or oatmeal $20–25, 4 7/8" dessert bowl $10–12.

Jane Ray cups and saucers. The regular Jane Ray cups and saucers are probably the most plentiful of all Fire-king pieces. Regular cup & saucer $8–10, demitasse cup & saucer $85–95, demitasse cup $50–55, demitasse saucer $35–40.

Decorated box for a Jane Ray starter set. This box is relatively common and one of the few Jadite-related decorated boxes. Condition greatly affects price. $30–60.

Jane Ray sugar and creamer.
Sugar with cover $25–30,
creamer $12–15.

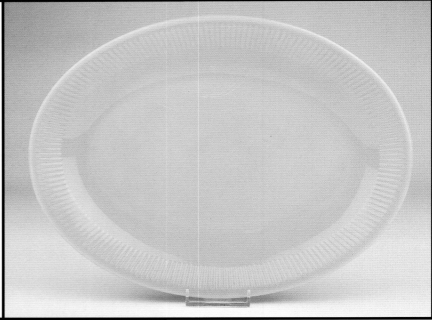

Jane Ray 9" x 12"
platter. $30–35.

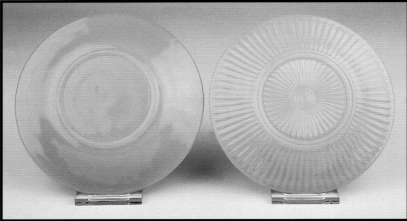

Underside of Jane Ray saucers.
The saucer with rays is more
difficult to find. Its cup ring is
slightly larger than the saucer
with plain back. $2–3 each.

Regular Jane Ray cup (left), opalescent cup (right). The opalescent pieces turn up occasionally. The are actually factory mistakes that made it out of the factory to the marketplace. The current value greatly depends on the extent of the opalescence. This cup should retail at $30–40.

66

Jane Ray plates with vintage decals. Collectors report these with various decals. All were probably decorated after they left the factory. $15–25 each.

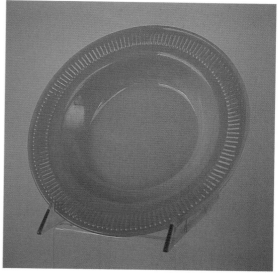

Jane Ray flanged soup bowl. Rare. $500–750.

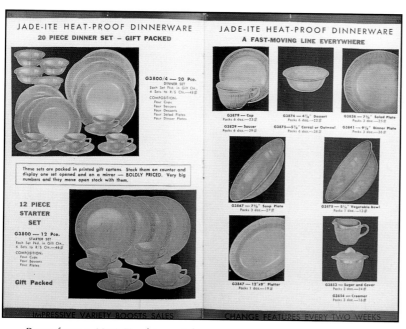

Pages from a 1953 Fire-king catalogue.

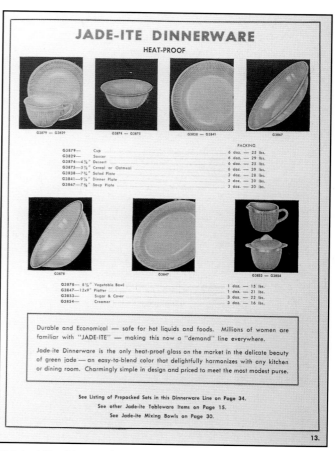

Original Fire-king catalogue advertisement.

Restaurant Ware

Although Restaurant Ware was produced for institutional use, it is currently the most popular of jadite dinnerware. A wide variety of pieces are available with enough serving and specialty pieces to appeal to both the practical buyer and the avid collector. Basic dinner pieces are expensive. This dinnerware was mass-produced and marketed in quantity. Most pieces were sold exclusively in cases that included dozens of pieces.

There are many sizes of plates, platters, cups and saucers, and bowls. Certain items like the 8" luncheon and the flat soup are scarce and virtually have disappeared from the secondary market. The small sandwich platters, with or without the indent, are extremely scarce. The three larger platters are more readily found, but still in great demand. The ball jug was advertised with the Restaurant Ware, but it neither matches the rest of the line in form or function. It is not a practical piece for institutional use, with its delicate handle. It is found, more frequently than not, with internal cracks where the handle joins the body of the jug. Even the ball jug in Anchor Hocking's morgue has these stress cracks. Similarly, this piece is much thinner than other Restaurant Ware pieces.

There are several pieces in this line that are extremely rare. The 10 1/2" dinner/serving plate photographed in this section is from the morgue. It was produced in 1949 and only a couple of examples have been reported. The large handled soup cup and saucer are also extremely rare. The cup is reminiscent of other Restaurant Ware, but the saucer is more like that of the 1700 line.

Different molds were used over the course of nearly 20 years that this line was produced. The earlier molds produced heavier pieces. This is especially true of dinner plates, where collectors tend to prefer the earlier pieces. The later dinner plates have a slightly beaded rim.

Restaurant plates. 10 3/8" (G317) large dinner or serving plate marked "Fire-king Oven Ware," $500+. 9" dinner plate, $25–30. 8" lunch plate, Rare, $50–60. 6 3/4" pie or salad plate, $10–12. 5 1/2" bread and butter plate, $12–15.

Morgue photo of rare 10 3/8" dinner. Dated 1949.

Backside of 2 Restaurant Pie plates. While these pieces have the same style number (G297), they are from totally different molds. The earlier plate on the left has a raised foot. Some collectors do not like mixing styles. Matching backstamps is usually a good way to maintain consistency.

Every Essential Item for Food Service Operations

JADE-ITE HEAVY-DUTY RESTAURANT WARE

A Jade-ite installation will cut your dinnerware costs in half.

- SANITARY
- STAIN-PROOF
- HEAT-RESISTANT
- COLORFUL
- INEXPENSIVE

G299
7-oz. Cup

G295—6" Saucer

G215
6-oz. Cup

G212
7-oz. Mug

G319
6-oz. Cup

G309
10-oz. Bowl

G294
4¾" Fruit Dish

G300
15-oz. Bowl

G307—9½" Oval Platter

G315—5½"
Bread & Butter Plate

G297—6¾" Pie-Salad Plate

G306—9" Dinner Plate

G308—11½" Oval Platter

G292—9½" Compartment Plate

Millions of pieces of Jade-ite Restaurant Ware are now used by the restaurant industry. It will pay you to change your service to JADE-ITE!

Pamphlet advertising Restaurant Ware. From Anchor Hocking company records.

69

Cardboard box for Fire-king Restaurant plates. $10–15.

Restaurant bowls. Clockwise from left. 15-ounce bowl beaded rim (G300), $40–45. 9" rim soup bowl (G298), $125–150. 8-ounce cereal with flanged lip (G305), $30–35. Chili bowl (not part of restaurant line), $12–15. 10-ounce bowl (G309) with beaded rim, $40–45. 4 3/4" fruit bowl (G294), $12–15.

Above: Comparison of the 10-ounce and 15-ounce bowls.

Right: Restaurant rimmed soup bowl. $125–150.

Fire-king handled
soup cup and saucer.
Extremely rare.
$1000–1200.

Restaurant cups and saucers.
Clockwise from top. Extra
Heavy cup (G299) and
saucer, $12–15. 7-ounce
tapered cup (G207) and
saucer, $30–35. Demitasse
cup and saucer, $100–125.
6-ounce tall cup (G215) and
saucer, $15–18.

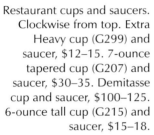

Comparison for size of the
St. Denis cup and saucer
and the handled soup cup.
The saucer to the soup cup
is a larger version of the St.
Denis saucer.

Restaurant Mugs. There are three distinct
mugs. The slim chocolate or "cheater"
mug is in the center. It holds 6 ounces and
is considerably smaller than the others.
The mugs at either end (G212) hold 7
ounces. They differ in thickness and are
probably from different periods of Fire-
king production. The thickest mug is the
most popular. Chocolate mug $30–35,
extra-heavy mugs $25–28.

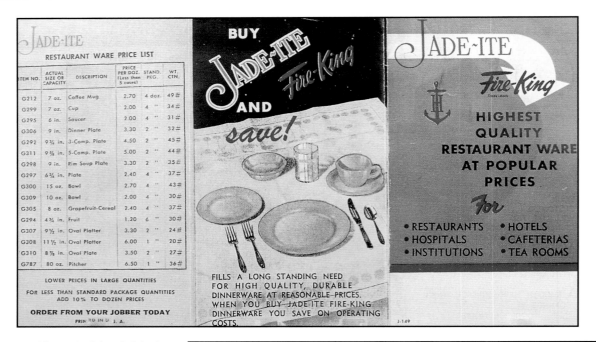

ITEM NO.	ACTUAL SIZE OR CAPACITY	DESCRIPTION	PRICE PER DOZ. (Less than 5 cases)	STAND. PKG.	WT. CTN.
G212	7 oz.	Coffee Mug	2.70	4 doz.	49#
G299	7 oz.	Cup	2.00	4 "	34#
G295	6 in.	Saucer	2.00	4 "	31#
G306	9 in.	Dinner Plate	3.30	2 "	32#
G292	9¾ in.	3-Comp. Plate	4.50	2 "	45#
G311	9⅝ in.	5-Comp. Plate	5.00	2 "	44#
G298	9 in.	Rim Soup Plate	3.30	2 "	35#
G297	6¾ in.	Plate	2.40	4 "	37#
G300	15 oz.	Bowl	2.70	4 "	43#
G309	10 oz.	Bowl	2.00	4 "	30#
G305	8 oz.	Grapefruit-Cereal	2.40	4 "	37#
G294	4¾ in.	Fruit	1.20	6 "	30#
G307	9½ in.	Oval Platter	3.30	2 "	24#
G308	11½ in.	Oval Platter	6.00	1 "	20#
G310	8⅞ in.	Oval Plate	3.50	2 "	27#
G787	80 oz.	Pitcher	6.50	1 "	36#

LOWER PRICES IN LARGE QUANTITIES

FOR LESS THAN STANDARD PACKAGE QUANTITIES
ADD 10% TO DOZEN PRICES

ORDER FROM YOUR JOBBER TODAY

PRINTED IN U.S.A.

BUY **Jade-ite** AND **Fire-King** save!

FILLS A LONG STANDING NEED FOR HIGH QUALITY, DURABLE DINNERWARE AT REASONABLE PRICES. WHEN YOU BUY JADE-ITE FIRE-KING DINNERWARE YOU SAVE ON OPERATING COSTS.

Jade-ite Fire-King

HIGHEST QUALITY RESTAURANT WARE AT POPULAR PRICES

For

- RESTAURANTS
- HOTELS
- HOSPITALS
- CAFETERIAS
- INSTITUTIONS
- TEA ROOMS

J-149

Above & right: Original Restaurant Ware brochure. Notice the inclusion of the ball jug. One dozen for $6.50!

HEAT PROOF . . . RESTAURANT DINNERWARE . . .

Jade-ite Fire-King

HEAT PROOF · · · JUST LIKE FAMOUS FIRE KING OVEN-WARE.

YOUR CUSTOMERS WILL LIKE THIS DINNERWARE SERVICE — THE ONLY DINNERWARE AVAILABLE IN THE DELICATE COLOR OF GREEN JADE THAT HARMONIZES SO DELIGHTFULLY WITH ANY SETTING · · ·

A SMOOTH HARD SURFACE WHICH CANNOT BE EFFECTED BY HOT FOODS OR LIQUIDS

DESIGNED TO GIVE THE UTMOST SATISFACTION WHERE SPEED OF SERVICE IS IMPORTANT · · ·

Restaurant platters.

Jadite ball jug. Scarce. Difficult to find without stress cracks by the handle. $700–$800. Ball jugs with stress cracks seem to consistently sell in the $250–300 price range.

Right: Oval platters. 11 1/2" Oval platter (G308) $60–65, 9 1/2" oval platter (G307) $50–55.

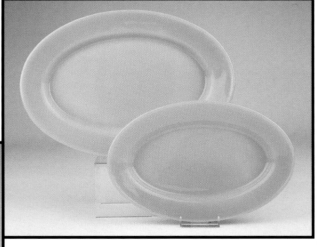

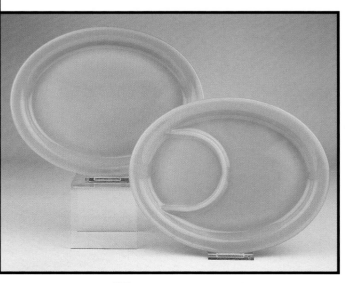

Above: 8 7/8" Oval plate, non-partitioned, $150–160. 9 3/4" football platter, $85–95.

Right: 8 7/8" oval plates. Partitioned (G211) $100–110, non-partitioned $150–160. The partitioned plate holds the 10-ounce (G309) bowl.

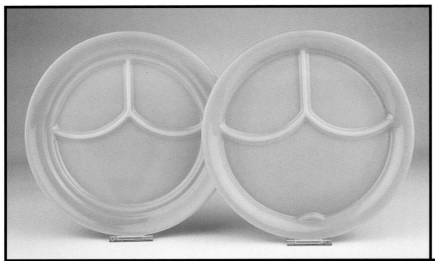

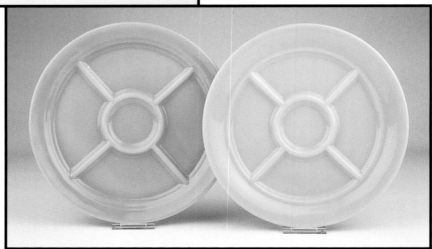

Above: 9 3/4" Restaurant grill plate, 3 compartments (G292). Comes with or without tab. The tab helps to keep these plates balanced when stacking. $25–30 each.

Right: 9 5/8" Restaurant 5-compartment plate (G311). 2 styles. $35–40. each.

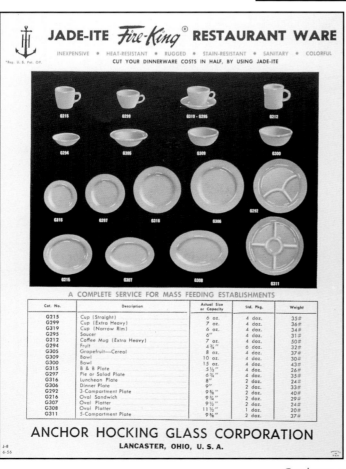

Catalogue advertisements.

Rare Fire-king gravy with restaurant cup
for size comparison. Gravy $2000–2500.

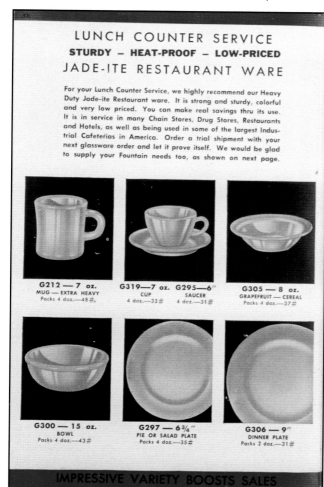

LUNCH COUNTER SERVICE
STURDY – HEAT-PROOF – LOW-PRICED
JADE-ITE RESTAURANT WARE

For your Lunch Counter Service, we highly recommend our Heavy
Duty Jade-ite Restaurant ware. It is strong and sturdy, colorful
and very low priced. You can make real savings thru its use.
It is in service in many Chain Stores, Drug Stores, Restaurants
and Hotels, as well as being used in some of the largest Industrial Cafeterias in America. Order a trial shipment with your
next glassware order and let it prove itself. We would be glad
to supply your Fountain needs too, as shown on next page.

G212 — 7 oz.
MUG — EXTRA HEAVY
Packs 4 doz.—48 #

G319—7 oz.
CUP
4 doz.—32 #

G295—6"
SAUCER
4 doz.—31 #

G305 — 8 oz.
GRAPEFRUIT — CEREAL
Packs 4 doz.—37 #

G300 — 15 oz.
BOWL
Packs 4 doz.—43 #

G297 — 6¾"
PIE OR SALAD PLATE
Packs 4 doz.—35 #

G306 — 9"
DINNER PLATE
Packs 2 doz.—31 #

IMPRESSIVE VARIETY BOOSTS SALES

1953 catalogue advertisement. Notice the 15-ounce
bowl is included. Perhaps this explains why this bowl
is found more frequently than the 10-ounce bowl.

Restaurant dinner plate with handpainted
holly, dated 1978. Dozens of these have
turned up in Ohio and Indiana. $30–35.

1700 Line and Breakfast Set

The 1700 line and the breakfast set contain several of the same pieces and thus are included together here. The 1700 line is a small line of dinnerware that includes several of the same pieces as the Jane Ray dinner line, with the difference being that the 1700 line lacks the ridges that decorate Jane Ray. This has caused collectors to name it "Plain Jane." The pieces that closely mimic Jane Ray include the cereal, soup, and dinner plate. This line also includes two styles of cups and saucers.

In addition to the plate, cup, and saucer listed above, the breakfast set includes the 20-ounce milk pitcher, the double egg cup, and the 16-ounce breakfast bowl. The breakfast bowl can be found with red ivy trim. The pitcher also comes decorated with beaded swirls and is referred to by collectors as the "Bead and Bar" pitcher. It is considerably more scarce than the plain pitcher.

The 1700 line and the breakfast set pieces can be found in other Fire-king colors including white, ivory, and peach lustre. This line includes additional pieces other than those found in jadite, including a platter, a salad plate, and a serving bowl. Perhaps these will turn up in jadite, too.

Above: 1700 dinner plate. This plate is larger than the restaurant dinner and is often confused with the thinner of the two restaurant dinners. This plate is thin and does not have a beaded edge. Scarce. $35–40.

Right: Fire-king Breakfast set.

Breakfast plate with label. Label adds $2–3 to the piece.

Breakfast cups and saucers. Left: Ransom cup and saucer, $25–30. Right: St. Denis cup and saucer, $12–15.

Double egg cups from Breakfast Set. $40–45.

Breakfast bowls. 16-ounce azurite with red ivy, $60–70. Ivory with green ivy, $50–55. Plain jadite, $100–125. Jadite with red ivy, $125–150.

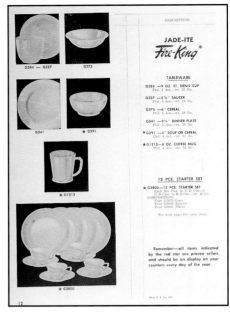

Right: Fire-king 1700 line cereal and soup bowl. Cereal bowl $50–55, soup bowl $65–75.

Far right: Fire-king catalogue advertisement for some 1700 line pieces.

Sheaves of Wheat

"Sheaves of Wheat" is another Anchor Hocking Fire-king line that was limited in variety of pieces and quantity of production. Its name was given by collectors years ago, some of whom call it "Sheath of Wheat" or "Sheaf of Wheat." The only company information that we were able to locate indicates that the pattern was simply called "Wheat." Fire-king had a later dinnerware and ovenware line that was also called "Wheat," which only adds to the confusion.

This pattern was produced in an extremely limited line in jadite and crystal, with only four pieces being produced in jadite. The morgue pieces indicate that these jadite items were manufactured in 1957 and 1958. All pieces of jadite are scarce, with the dessert bowl being the most difficult to find. The dinner plate has the thickness of Jane Ray and is decorated with the wheat design around he border. It is one of the most attractive of the jadite dinnerware pieces. This line would be extremely popular if more of it were available.

Sheaves of Wheat dinnerware.

Sheaves of Wheat 9″ dinner plate. Scarce. $75–85.

Close-up of the wheat design.

Above: Sheaves of Wheat 4 1/2″ dessert bowl. $100–125.

Right: Sheaves of Wheat cup and saucer. Scarce. Cup $40–50, saucer $15–20.

Shell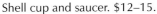

Shell was produced from the mid-1960s until the mid-1970s. The dinnerware has a scalloped edge and a swirled design. It is often confused with the more rare Swirl dinnerware.

Jadite Shell could be purchased in a twelve piece starter set that included dinner plates, cups, and saucers. Other available pieces could be purchased open stock. This explains the difficulty collectors have in obtaining enough salad plates, bowls, and platters to complete their sets. Creamers and sugars are not difficult to find, but the lid to the sugar is scarce. Shell can also be found in white, gold trimmed white, peach lustre, and iridized mother-of-pearl.

The oval vegetable pictured in this section was produced by Anchor Hocking but we have been unable to locate any documentation that would prove its inclusion in either the Shell or Swirl dinnerware lines. Very few of these bowls have been found in jadite, however they can be found in Anchor Hocking's Royal Ruby and Forest Green.

Shell cup and saucer. $12–15.

Shell dinnerware.

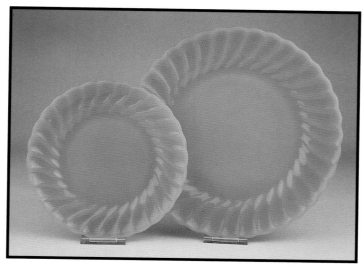

Above: Shell plates. The Shell dinner has a large flat center. It is the largest of the Fire-king dinner plates. 7 1/4" salad plate $15–20, 10" dinner $22–25.

Right: Shell bowls. 8" vegetable bowl $30–35, 7 5/8" soup plate $30–35, 6 3/8" cereal bowl $25–30, 4 3/4" dessert bowl $12–15.

jade-ite
dinnerware

heat-resistant; a long-time best seller, now in new swirled English Regency style

G2379	8 oz cup • 3 dz/shipper/14 lbs
G2329	5¾" saucer • 3 dz/shipper/13 lbs
G2374	4¾" dessert • 3 dz/shipper/13 lbs
G2338	7¼" salad plate • 3 dz/shipper/23 lbs
G2367	6⅜" soup • 3 dz/shipper/22 lbs

G2346	10" dinner plate • 3 dz/shipper/43 lbs
G2378	8½" vegetable • 1 dz/shipper/14 lbs
G2347	13" x 9½" platter • 1 dz/shipper/22 lbs
G2353	sugar/cover • 1 dz/shipper/9 lbs
G2354	creamer • 1 dz/shipper/6 lbs
G2300/5	12 pc starter set • gift ctn • 6 sets/shipper/49 lbs
	4 cups • 4 saucers • 4 dinner plates
G2300/13	45 pc set • 1 set/shipper/30 lbs
	8 cups • 8 saucers • 8 desserts • 8 soups •
	8 dinner plates • vegetable • platter •
	sugar/cover • creamer

20

1963 Fire-king catalogue advertisement.

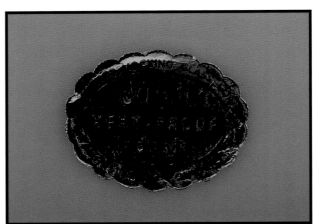

Shell dinner plate with label.

Shell oval vegetable. Company catalogues do not list this piece. It does not strictly match the design of the other shell pieces, but the scalloped edges are reminiscent of this pattern. Rare. $500–1000.

Shell tid-bit. There is no mention in company literature of this piece being produced at the factory. This one was made from a saucer, salad plate, and dinner plate. It could have been made at any time after production. We know of dealers who currently make them. $50–75.

Shell sugar and creamer. The sugar cover is difficult to find. Sugar bowl with cover $65–75, sugar cover $45–50, creamer $20–25.

Swirl

Anchor Hocking's Swirl dinnerware is an extremely limited line that is seldom found. We were very excited to discover a jadite swirl platter in the morgue at Anchor Hocking. This platter was most likely a prototype that never went in to regular production. Only time will tell how many more, if any, will turn up! Until this discovery, only cups, saucers, and dinner plates had been found in jadite swirl. A complete line of Swirl was made in azurite, white, ivory, pink, and rose-ite.

Swirl dinnerware.

Swirl dinner plate.
Scarce item. $75–85.

Swirl cup &
saucer. Scarce
item. $75–85.

Rare Fire-king swirl
platter from the
morgue. $500+.

Above: Rose-ite swirl dinnerware from the morgue. NV.

Left: Magazine advertisement for pink Swirl dinnerware.

Children's Pieces and Demitasse Cups & Saucers

Inexpensively produced children's dishes that match regular dinnerware were frequently produced during the Depression era. McKee's Laurel children's set is the only example of a jadite children's set made to match regular sized dishes.

The Fire-king children's plate and mug are exceptionally rare and command very high prices. These were made for children to use rather than for play. The mug is slightly shorter than the commonly found 8-ounce mug and has a flat bottom.

Fire-king demitasse cups and saucers were technically created for after-dinner coffee, but were also used as children's dishes. Surely most diners and institutions that used Restaurant Ware were not using these items.

The swirl demi cup and saucer is from Argentina. We have not heard of other jadite pieces in this line, but have found the demi cup and saucer in custard as well.

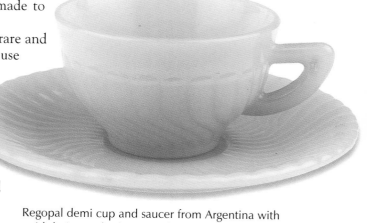

Regopal demi cup and saucer from Argentina with swirl design on both cup and saucer. We have found a similar demi cup and saucer in custard. We have no information about what else may have been made.

Above: Demitasse cups and saucers. From left: Restaurant demi cup and saucer, $100–125. Jane Ray demi cup and saucer, $90–100. Regopal demi cup and saucer (from Argentina), $125–150.

Left: Close-up of Regopal backstamp.

Jadite demi cup and saucer. Unidentified. $75–100.

Weston or Akro Agate demitasse cup and saucer. No markings. Akro Agate acquired Weston molds after company burned down in 1936. $18–20.

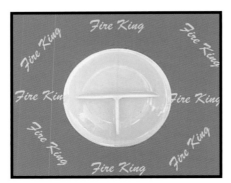

Fire-king child's mug. This mug is slightly shorter than the common Fire-king mug. It is extremely scarce and highly sought after. $650–750.

Fire-king jadite children's plate. Very rare. $1200–$1750.

Fire-king demitasse cups from the morgue. $300+ each.

Akro Agate Raised Daisy cup. Scarce. A full line of Akro Agate children's dishes was produced in colors similar to Jadite, though usually a bit darker. We have not included these dishes in this book. Several books on this topic are widely available.

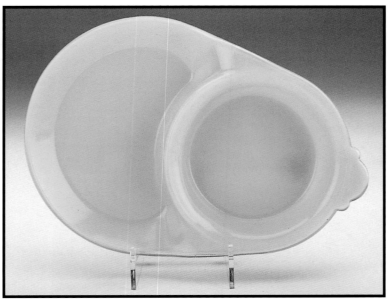

McKee baby's feeding dish or snack tray. Rare. $400–500.

McKee eggbeater bowl. We have found several of these with children's size utensils. Bowl with beater $40–45. Bowl alone $20–25.

Hostess set for children. Original ad.

Laurel children's dishes.

Additional Dinnerware

All jadite dinnerware was not made in easy to define patterns. Numerous pieces were made as accessory items by Fire-king, McKee, and other companies. Some of these pieces compliment other lines, like the thin Fire-king mugs. Other pieces, like the McKee Tom and Jerry punch bowl set, were made as occasional items.

The thin Fire-king mugs present a problem for many collectors. Lacking company documentation, collectors have assigned names to the mugs to differentiate one from another. The Philbe mug is the easiest to identify. It has the Philbe pattern on the side. The mug that is identical to the Philbe mug without design is called the plain Philbe or the Philbe "wannabe" (want to be). This mug is also scarce. It has a pronounced ring at the base. The shaving mug has a perfectly flat bottom. And finally, there is the common 8-ounce mug.

The Fire-king Laurel cup is from the morgue. We have heard of no examples turning up in the marketplace, but surely more than one was made. The round Fire-king bowl is believed to be a one-of-a-kind piece that turned up in the Lancaster area. No company information exists on it.

The Pyrex dinnerware set is fired-on green. A full line was made including plates, bowls, and serving pieces.

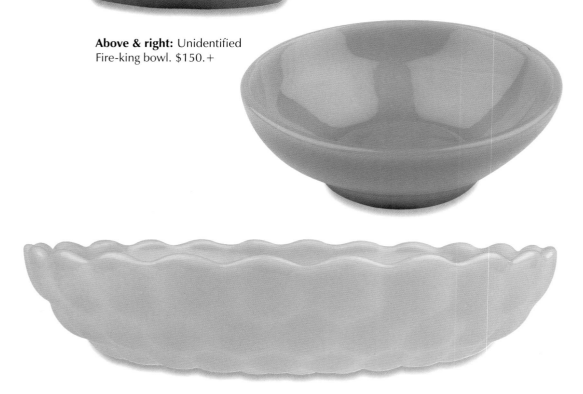

Above & right: Unidentified Fire-king bowl. $150.+

Above: Bubble Bowl. The only piece of this popular Anchor Hocking pattern to be found in jadite. This pattern is usually found in light blue, forest green, and royal ruby. Jadite bowl, $20–22.

Right: Fire-king 5″ straight sided bowl. $50–60.

McKee Flower band items. Only these two pieces were produced in this line. Footed tumbler $18–20, 9 1/2" bowl with 6 triangular feet $45–50.

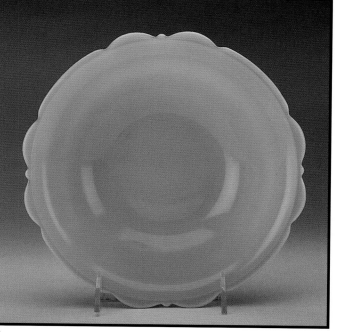

McKee scalloped serving bowl. $25–30.

Ten-sided bowl with ground bottom. This bowl is better quality glass than most jadite. $75–100.

McKee 10-sided handled plate and bowl. 11" plate $50–55, 9" bowl $50–55.

Jadite sugar and creamer. $75–100 set.

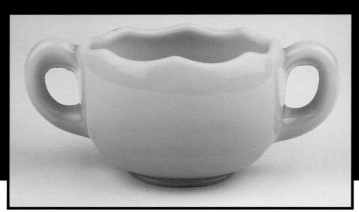

Jadite sugar. $20–25.

Fire-king Laurel cup. This item is from the morgue. $250.+

Fire-king thin mugs. Regular 8-ounce mug $10–12, shaving mug with flat bottom $15–18, plain Philbe mug $30–35, Philbe mug $125–150.

Close-up of Philbe and plain Philbe mugs.

Above: McKee Tom and Jerry Punch Set. Punch bowl $125–150, mug $30–35.

Right: Different styles of printing on Tom and Jerry mugs.

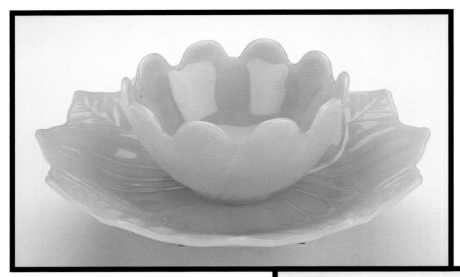

Fire-king Leaf and Blossom
snack set. $25–30.

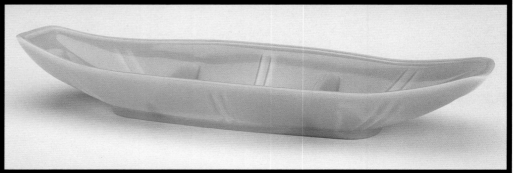

Jadite divided relish. $40–50.

Jadite two-tiered serving
dish. $100–125.

McKee Lenox divided celery, $40–45. A few other
pieces of McKee's Lenox line were made in jadite.

Jadite toothpick. $30–35.

Jeannette egg cup, $20–25. McKee custard, $20–25.

McKee coaster set. Container $125–150, plain coasters $25–30 each.

McKee coasters, ribbed. $30–40 each.

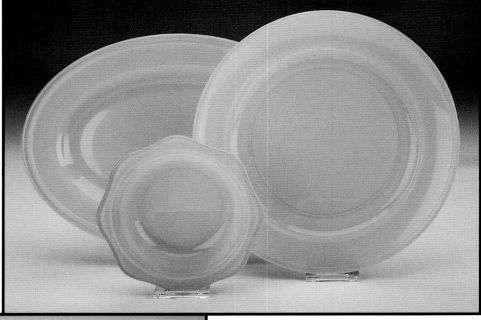

Pyrex fired-on green dinnerware. Other pieces exist in this line. 6" cereal bowl, $12–15. 10" dinner plate, $15–18. Platter, $20–25.

Fired-on green sugar and creamer $20–25.

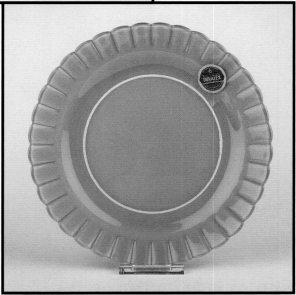

French fired-on green plate by Duralex. $12–15.

Jadite Throughout the Home

Advertising Jadite

The light green opaque color of jadite dishes created a perfect medium for advertisements. Both red and black print were used on household and bar-related items to advertise a variety of products.

A group of ashtrays were produced by the RegiCor Company in England to advertise beer and soft drinks. These items closely resemble the thickness and color of Fire-king jadite. We have not found any non-advertising items or dinnerware from this company.

Two McKee bowls were used to advertise supermarkets. While we have not heard of any Jeannette jadite that was used for advertising, numerous Fire-king dishes were decorated to advertise all sorts of products. Some of these are simply Fire-king items to which something was added—a decal, some paint, or a metal lid. These items are less sought-after than factory decorated items like the Steering mug and the Puro ball pitcher.

Souvenir items were all decorated after they left the factory. The 1998 Tulsa mug, for example, was made by decorating a vintage mug for the Fire-king Expo. The chili golf classic bowl was similarly decorated long after the item was produced.

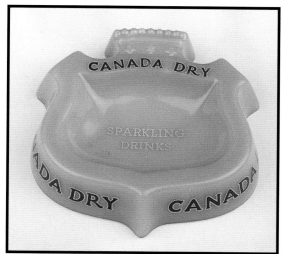

Canada Dry advertising ashtray (marked on back: RegiCor Made In England). $100–125.

Above: English jadite. 6 1/2" Plate "Souvenir of London".$30–40. Whiteways Devon Cyder advertising ashtray, marked RegiCor on reverse. $45–50.

Right: RegiCor ashtrays. Beefeater Gin $45–50, Tennent's Beer $45–50.

Mitre Scotch Whiskey ashtray. $45–50.

Texaco ashtray for automobile. Scarce. $150–175.

Fire-king 10-ounce bowl decorated for the "Chili Open Golf Classic" 1977. $45–50.

Above: Chili bowl with metal advertising cover. These can be found with many different company names embossed on the cover. $20–25.

Left: McKee scalloped bowl advertising the Austin Piggly Wiggly. $125–150.

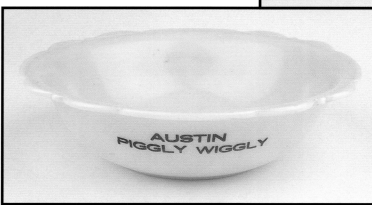

McKee 9" bell shaped bowl advertising
"J. Grosso Market, Leechburg, Pa." $150–200.

Fired-on green
child's cereal bowl
advertising the
cowboy Bobby
Benson. $30–40.

Above: Fire-king Restaurant demi cup and saucer
advertising Northwestern Bottle Company. This is
a decal applied to the cup. We have seen this in
ivory as well. In jadite, $125–150.

Right: Hand painted Fire-king restaurant demi
cup. Souvenir of the Ozarks. $75–85.

Advertising Fire-king mugs. Left to right: Niagara Falls mug $20–25, Saginaw
Steering Gear 1958 Restaurant mug $75–85, Masonic Restaurant mug $45–50.

A mug specially decorated for the
1998 Fire-king expo in Tulsa. NV

Jane Ray saucer with decal that states, "Special Offer!
Start your set today with each purchase of 25 lb.
Pillsbury's best flour." Scarce. $35–40.

Fire-king ball jug
advertising Puro
filtered water. Rare.
$2000–2500.

Ashtrays

Several companies besides Jeannette, McKee, and Anchor Hocking made jadite ashtrays in a variety of shapes and sizes. Most of the ashtrays we find with advertising were produced in England and most likely were picked up by tourists.

The Frankart Co. and Nuart Metal Creation Co. commissioned jadite ashtrays and inserts to go with their white metal composition products.

Of particular interest is the photograph of the two square ashtrays. We found the smaller of the two in the morgue at Anchor Hocking. Although the larger ashtray is commonly found, we had never seen the small ashtray before. No documentation on the small ashtray could be located at Anchor Hocking, which leads us to believe it may have been a prototype that never went in to production.

Please refer to the advertising section for additional information about ashtrays.

Ashtray with cigarette holder of man driving a boat. Metal and jadite. ca.1930. $75–100.

Above: Ashtrays. McKee 7 1/2"ashtray with 5 circles in center, $75–85. 6" Nuart Metal Creations, made to fit in decorative metal holder, $40–50. 5" ashtray marked "APT NY" $30–35.

Right: Fire-king ashtrays. Small 3 1/2" square, from the morgue, NV. 4 1/4" square ashtray, $35-40.

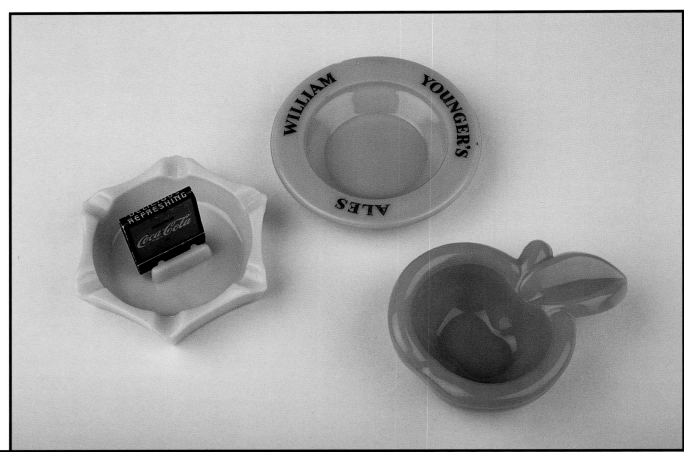

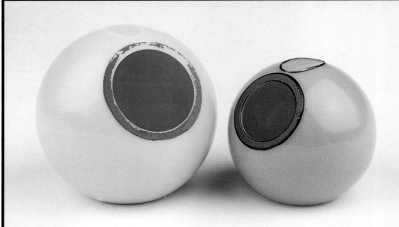

Above: Ashtrays. Jeannette hexagonal ashtray, $20–25. RegiCor advertising ashtray for William Younger's Ale, $45–50. Apple ashtray, $25–30.

Left: Ball-shaped ashtrays. Large 3 3/8", small 2 3/4". $60–70 each.

Below: Jadite ashtray. $20–25

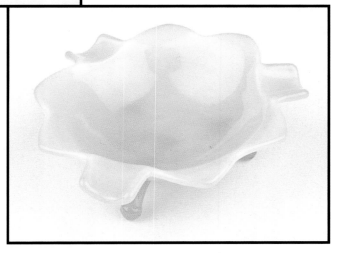

Bathroom and Barber Items

With the exception of the towel bars and the Akro Agate powder jar, most of the items in this section are scarce. Demand for these items, however, does not rise to the level of that for the scarce dinnerware and kitchenware. For the most part, these items are still reasonably priced.

The McKee barber bottles are exceptionally scarce. They were made from an old McKee bitters bottle mold. The sterilizer jar and cover is rarely seen and usually lacks the cover.

The Jeannette toilet set consisted of 4 bottles and a tumbler. The bottles are the same as the commonly found Jeannette shakers. They were marketed with black bakelite lids and are frequently found with small painted flowers.

The towel bars are found in a variety of sizes from 8" to 22" with a variety of metal and ceramic brackets. These towel bars were heavily produced in crystal. Thus, it is fairly easy to replace brackets for jadite towel bars with the more commonly found vintage brackets for the crystal bars.

Several companies made perfumes and cosmetic related jadite items. Expect to find many items that are not pictured here.

Above: McKee 6 5/8" barber bottle, Shampoo. $700–800.

Left: McKee 6 5/8" barber bottles. Toilet water and water, $700–800 each. Bottle without lettering, $200–250.

Bathroom bottles with black plastic cover and a black glass tray. This set is darker than most jadite. Individual bottles, $75–100. Complete set, $400–450.

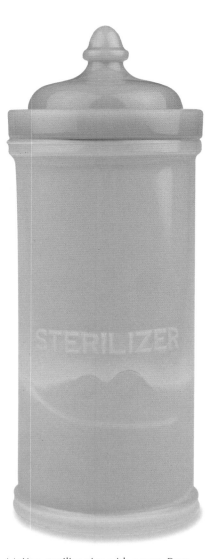

McKee sterilizer jar with cover. Rare. Cover is extremely rare. With cover $1000–1200, without cover $600–800.

Above & right: Powder jars and cosmetic containers. Left: Covered powder jar. Patent no. 1,692,310. $100–125. Right: Powder and cosmetic container with floral design on lid, $125–150.

New Martinsville clambroth perfume and puff boxes with black lids. Perfume $40–45, Puff box $30–35. Jadite 4 3/8" x 7" cosmetics tray, $50–60.

Light green jadite atomizer. $40–45.

3 1/2" perfume bottle. $50–75.

Clambroth cologne. $35–40.

Jadite cosmetic containers. With or without gold trim. $45–50.

Above: Morgantown thin 4″ cosmetics box with "Leda with the swan" decoration. $50–60.

Left: Akro Agate vertical rib powder jar. $25–30.

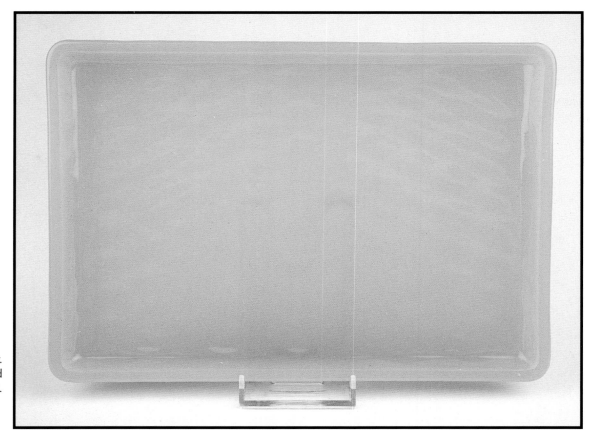

Light jadite tray. Diamond pattern. $50–60.

Jeannette bathroom set. Scarce. Boric Acid, Mouth Wash, and Epsom Salt containers, $200–250 each. Bathroom tumbler, $80–90.

Above: Jeannette 5" x 5" leftover with "SOAP" in black letters. We are not sure of the vintage of the lettering. NV

Left: Bi-carbonate soda shaker. Part of the 5-piece bathroom set by Jeannette. These shakers are considered rare. $200–250.

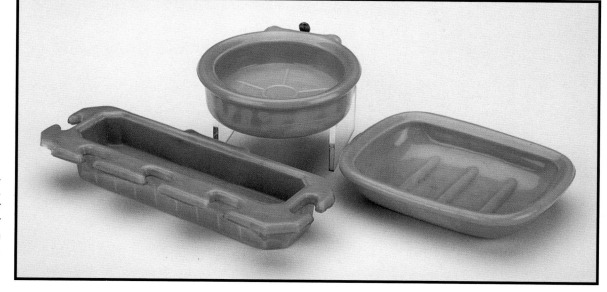

Bathroom pieces, dark jadite. Toothbrush holder $20–25, cup holder $15–20, soap dish $15–20.

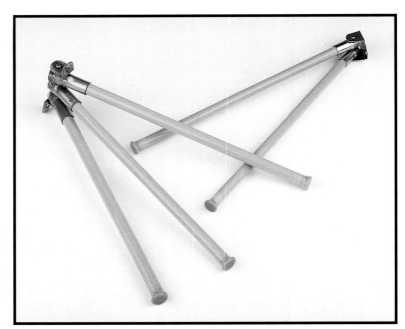

Jadite towel bars. 3 bars with metal clasp, $50–60. 2 bars, $40–50.

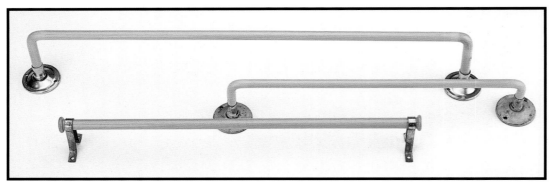

Jadite towel bars with metal brackets. 17" towel bar, $40–45. 15" towel bar, $35–40. 22" towel bar, $65–75.

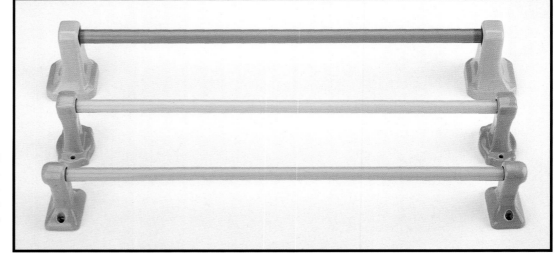

Jadite towel bars with ceramic brackets. Light and dark jadite. 18"–19" towel bars, $45–50.

Jadite shelf. 4" x 16". $100–125.

Candy Dishes, Comports, and Console Sets

Most of the items featured in this section have not been very difficult to find in recent years, but with the increased popularity of jadite, we expect that these items will also rapidly disappear from the market. Several of these items, like the Maple Leaf and shell candy dishes, were given away or sold cheaply as part of promotions.

Of special interest is the Anchor Hocking shell-shaped dish with the inwardly curved tab handle. This unique item was either a prototype or an employee's lunch-time project. It was found in the Lancaster, Ohio area.

Above: Fire-king candy dishes and comports. From left: Leaf candy dish also given away as a spoon rest, $20–25. Shell candy dish, $25–30. 6" comport, $75–85.

Left: Fire-king shell candy dish with turned-in handle. Possibly an end-of-day or experimental piece. $250+.

Candy dishes and bulb bowls. Clockwise from left. 6" Bulb bowl or candy dish with straight rim, $20–25. 6" Diamond bottom bowl with straight rim, $30–35. 6 1/2" diamond bottom bowl with ruffled rim, scarce, $70–80. 7" swirled bowl with ruffled edge, $45–50.

Fire-king covered candy dish. Watch for nicks on points of cover. $75–85.

Jewel boxes. Fired-on green with white vitrock cover, $20–25. Jadite box with jadite cover, $60–65.

Fire-king jadite jewel box and fired-on green puff box with white cover. Jewel box $60–65, puff box $20–25.

Fire-king three-footed bulb bowl $25–30.

Above: Light jadite chicken on a nest. $40–50

Left: Fire-king advertisement for "Miscellaneous Glassware."

Candy comports and epergne. 2 piece epergne $75–85, candy comports $30–35 each.

McKee console set.
Comport, 3 1/2″ x
5 1/2″, $40–45.
Comport, 5 1/2″ x
8 1/2″, $50–60.
Candlesticks,
$60–70 pair.

Clambroth
console set.
$75–100.

Above: Clambroth bowls and ashtray. Console
bowls $30–40 each. Ashtray $20–25.

Left: McKee floral candles with hand-painted
decorations. $70–80.

Kitchen Appliances

The abundance of early electric mixers seen at flea markets and tag sales indicates that these labor-saving appliances were a great success. They easily could be adapted to perform many tedious food preparation tasks for the homemaker. The jadite mixing bowls and juicer attachments that came with them appear even more frequently than the mixers, indicating that the jadite bowls were used long after the electric mixers ceased to work.

Though not jadite, the green Hamilton Beach stick blenders and plastic ice-crusher are welcome decorative accents in many jadite collectors' kitchens.

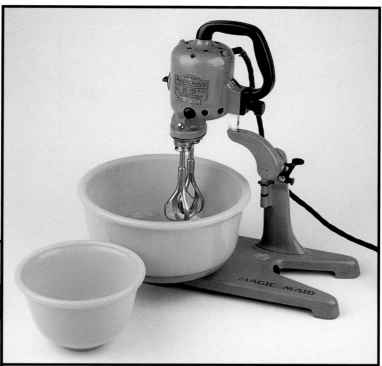

Magic Maid Mixer with reamer attachments. $80–100.

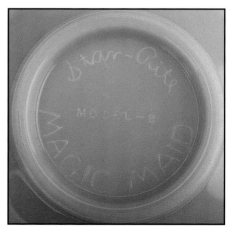

Magic Maid backstamps advertising different distributors.

Sunbeam Mix Masters with various attachments. Complete set $80–100.

Sunbeam Mix
Master brochures.
$10–15 each

HOW
TO GET THE MOST
OUT OF YOUR
MIXMASTER

★

NOW
THAT
YOU
HAVE
YOUR
AUTOMATIC
MIXMASTER

MAKE it save you all the arm-work and time and give you all the marvelous results possible. Be sure you get all the good out of it that you can, because you can't overwork the Automatic Mixmaster.

Women who own the Mixmaster tell us the more they use it the more helpful it becomes, and the more they enjoy it. They say that scarcely a week passes but what they find some *new* way to make cooking, baking and getting the meals easier and better. You'll find that's true, too.

But do not limit the usefulness of the sturdy, powerful Mixmaster to just your mixing and beating work. Especially when at such a small cost you

can enlarge its usefulness and make it take over more and more of the disagreeable part of your kitchen work—leaving you just the fun and pleasure. That's one of the big Mixmaster advantages, and is probably one of the very reasons you chose Mixmaster in the first place.

And that's the purpose of this book—to help you get the most out of your Automatic Mixmaster.

In the forepart of this book the attachments you can get for your Mixmaster are illustrated. Each one makes short work of some hard or tiresome home task. All of them are practical and safe and substantial. They do their work much easier and quicker and better than it ever could be done by hand, or with any similar mechanical device, for that is the first rigid rule by which we judge each one before we offer it.

Mixmaster attachments are built to last and are simple to operate. They are items of kitchen equipment that you will use most every day, and that they quickly pay for themselves many times over in the food, time, work they save.

You can get those attachments from the dealer who sold you the Automatic Mixmaster. He will be glad to show them to you and sell you about them. So why not plan to add one attachment at a time until you have them all? With them you'll get the most out of your Automatic Mixmaster and be truly happy with it.

MIXMASTER
Is One of
THE *Sunbeam*
ELECTRIC APPLIANCES MADE
Made and guaranteed by
CHICAGO FLEXIBLE SHAFT CO.
5600 Roosevelt Road, Chicago, Ill.
47 Years Making Quality Products

113

Advertisement for Sunbeam accessories including a cabinet to hold all the different attachments.

1998 Postal Display for Sunbeam Mix Master stamp. "Give this stamp a whirl."

Handywhip mixer with jadite attachment. $50–55.

Handyhot juicit. Orange juice squeezer. $40–45.

114

Sunkist juicit. $60–65.

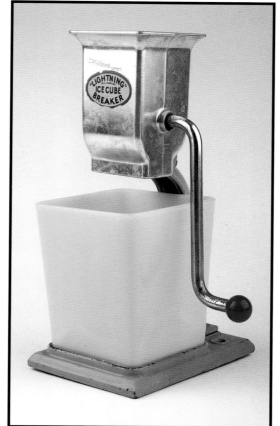

Lightning ice cube breaker with Jeannette canister base to catch ice. $70–80.

Above: Jeannette hand beater. $50–55.

Right: Jadite-colored mixers and ice crusher. Electric mixers, $75–150. Ice crusher, $30–35. Electric mixers have been made in "jadite" green since the 1930s and are still being made.

Lamps

Judging by the number of jadite lamps available today, they must have been a favorite in the 1930s. Several different companies produced lamps with jadite and clambroth parts. Most of these lamps were made of two or three different jadite pieces. The photos show several different lamps that used some of the same pieces. Four of the lamps pictured used the same octagonal base.

These lamps are currently a hard sell and are usually reasonably priced. Collectors prefer lamps that are composed mostly of jadite over those that have large exposed metal stems.

Clambroth bedroom lamps. $65–75 each.

Simple clambroth lamp. $50–60.

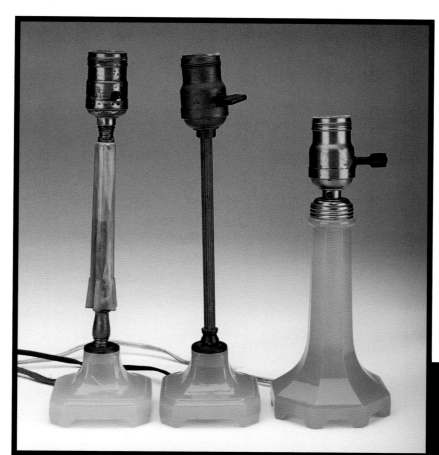

Lamps. Clambroth and bakelite, $75–100. Clambroth and metal, $50–60. Octagonal clambroth base, $60–70.

Jadite lamps. Octagonal base with jadite shade, $125–150. Octagonal base, $75–85. Jadite base and body, $100–125.

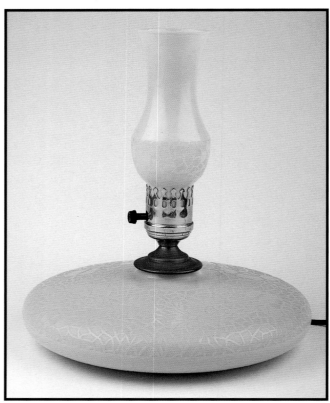

Above left: Jadite lamps. Octagonal base and body, $75–85. Jadite base and small disk, $50–60.

Above right: Jadite lamp with crackle design on base and shade. $175–200.

Right: Lamp with clambroth base and body. $125–150.

Far right: Jadite and bronze lamp. 22" tall. $150–175.

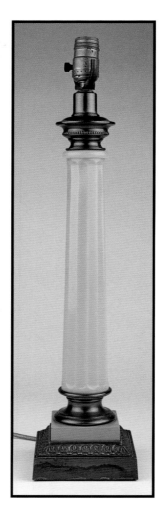

Clambroth lamp with
cylindrical shade. $125–150.

Dark jadite oil lamp. $150–175.

Jadite shade. $50–75.

Pitchers, Tumblers, and More

This section includes a broad array of pitchers and pouring items including water servers, decanters, and measuring cups. Many of these items are exceedingly rare and have disappeared into collections.

This grouping of Fire-king ball pitchers represents many of the most sought after jadite pieces. The Target, Swirl, advertising, and Manhattan-like jugs are very rare pieces that command a great deal of attention. Expect these pieces to be very expensive, if you are ever lucky enough to see one for sale. None of these items are in Anchor Hocking's morgue. The regular ball jug is a Fire-king favorite. They are more expensive than rare, with the demand keeping the prices high.

The McKee handleless pitcher and vinegar cruet are early examples of jadite. Early pre-jadite McKee catalogues show that the molds used for these items were used on colored glassware in the 1920s. The stopper for the vinegar cruet is exceedingly rare. Most examples of this item are found with a cork for a stopper, but company records show a glass stopper came with the cruet.

The Bottoms-up tumblers and the Bottoms-down mugs are a favorite with collectors. The spread-leg tumbler is much more scarce than the tumbler with legs together. It lacks the patent number that is found on the more frequently seen tumbler. Coasters are found with varying degrees of opalescence. Notice that the coaster photographed is quite translucent.

The water servers are extremely large and heavy. The clambroth water server with the crystal cover made by Sneath Glass Company is much more common than those made by McKee. The tall water server is very difficult to locate.

Fired-on green items that look like jadite have really started to take off, especially on the Internet. We have seen fired-on ball pitchers sell for more than $200. While that price cannot be sustained, the interest in fired-on pieces as a reasonable alternative to their jadite counterparts, has created considerable demand for these items.

Above: Fire-king Target ball jug. One of the most sought-after of all Fire-king pieces. Common in crystal. Very rare in jadite. $4000–5000+.

Right: Fire-king plain ball jug. Advertised in Restaurant Ware brochure, though clearly different thickness than most Restaurant Ware. Watch for internal cracks where the handle attaches to the ball jug. Even the pitcher in the morgue has this stress crack. In mint condition. $700–800.

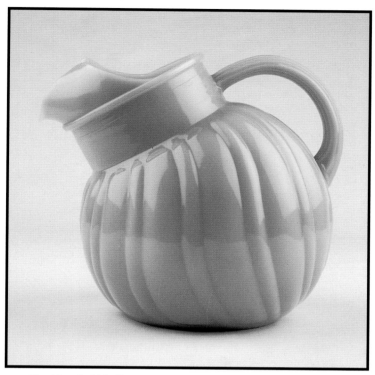

Fire-king Swirl ball jug. Extremely rare. $3000–4000.

Fire-king advertising ball jug for Puro water purifier. Rare. $2000–2500.

Jadite Manhattan-style ball jug. Note that the ribbing around the neck of the jadeite piece goes in the opposite direction from that on the Manhattan pitcher. Extremely rare. $3000–3500.

McKee Pinch water bottle and stopper. Very scarce. Stopper represents half of value. $325–350.

McKee handleless one-quart pitcher. Has liquid and dry measurements. 7 1/4". $1200–1500.

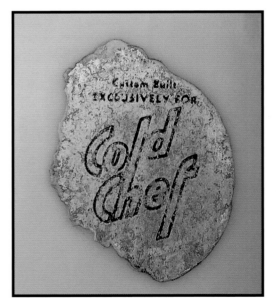

Cold Chef label on water bottle. Adds $50 to value.

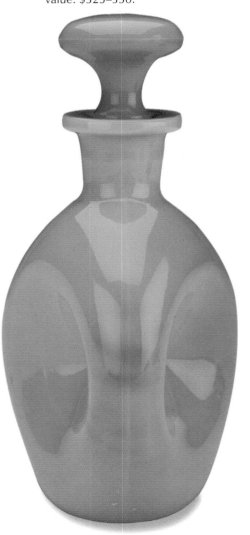

McKee pinch decanter with stopper. $375–400.

McKee water servers. Water server with round lid, $300–350. Tall water server with rectangular lid, $450–500.

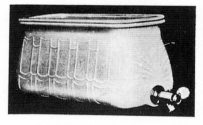
1933 ad for tall water server. From *Colored Glassware of the Depression Era, Book II* by Hazel Marie Weatherman.

McKee short water server with rectangular lid. This lid is interchangeable with that of the tall water server. $175–200.

Above & right: Sneath Glass Co. water server. Clambroth with round crystal lid. $80–100.

123

Above: Jeannette pitchers. Ice box jug and cover. $450–550. Pitcher, 33-ounce with sunflower base $75–85.

Right: Jeannette ice box jug and cover. Cover view.

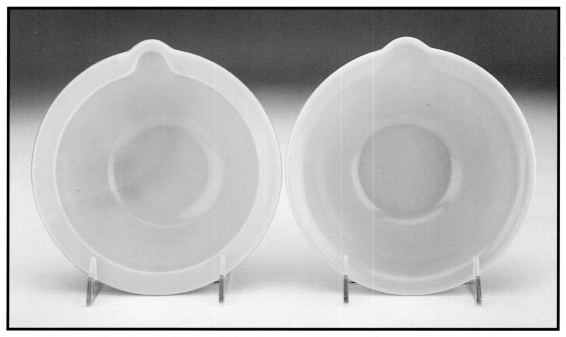

McKee batter bowls with two different style lips. $35–40 each.

Fire-king batter pitchers. Colonial batter pitcher with 1" band $50–60 (add $20 for the label). Batter pitcher with 3/4" band. $30–35.

Label for Colonial batter bowl.

Another Sensational **Anchorglass** Special
COMBINATION HANDLED MIXING-
BATTER BOWL — in Beautiful
HEAT-PROOF ··· JADE-ITE

Illustrated approximately four-fifths actual size.

G655—HANDLED BATTER BOWL
(Capacity 3½ Pints)
Pkd. 1 doz. ctn. — wt. 22 lbs.

Something new in Anchorglass kitchen bowls. This multiple-use bowl is designed for the most exacting housewife who demands the very best in everyday housewares.

TEST PROVEN BY TOP HOME ECONOMISTS! This perfect size bowl with its large firm-grip handle makes it truly a "non-slip" mixing bowl. The pouring lip is shaped to dispense thick or thin liquids without fear of over-pouring or drip-back. Ideal for mixing and pouring pancake batter, cake mixes, pie fillings, candies, etc. It can't be matched in price or beauty anywhere!

This label in each Bowl.

ANOTHER EXCELLENT PRODUCT BY ANCHOR HOCKING GLASS CORPORATION LANCASTER, OHIO, U.S.A.
New Handled
BATTER BOWL
with Pouring Lip
HEAT-PROOF
"Fire-King"
Ovenglass

4-56

Label inside Fire-king batter bowl.

Original advertisement for Fire-king batter bowl.

McKee 2-spout measuring cup. Scarce. $225–250.

Hocking one-cup measure in
Clambroth, 3 3/8". $200–225.

Hocking Clambroth 2-cup measuring
pitcher. $125–150.

McKee 4-cup measuring pitcher. $100–125.

McKee 2-cup measuring pitcher. $70–80.

Above: Fire-king pitchers. Left to right: Bead and Bar crystal $12–15, Bead and Bar jadite $225–250, jadite milk pitcher $75–85.

Right: Crystal and Jadite pitcher and tumbler set. Pitcher $125–150, tumblers $20–25 each.

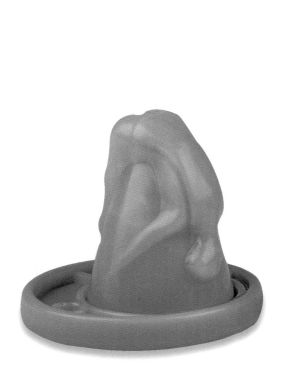

Bottoms-up cocktail tumbler with coaster and Bottoms-down handled beer mug. Both by McKee. ca. 1928–33. The handled mugs are quite scarce. Reproductions of the Bottoms-up have been made in a variety of colors. They are especially crude. The reproductions that we have seen do not have the patent number by the feet. Bottoms-up tumbler $75–100, bottoms-up coaster $150–175, Bottoms-down mug $300–350.

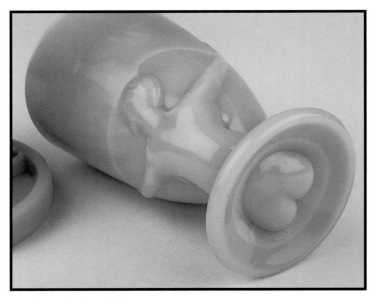

"Bottom" view of the mug.

McKee ad for bottoms down-mugs.

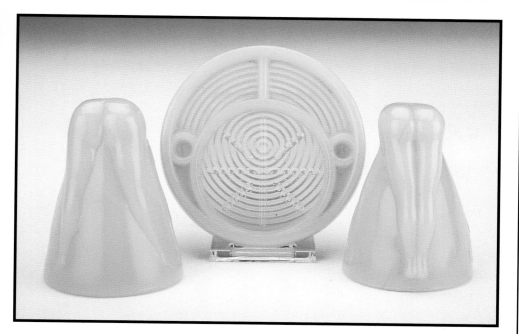

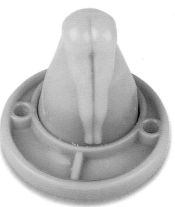

Above & right: Bottoms-up tumblers with coaster. The split-leg tumbler is considerably more difficult to locate than the tumbler with the legs together. Split leg tumbler, $200–250.

1932 ad for Bottoms-up tumblers. Notice that the tumblers were sold without the coaster, explaining the coasters' relative rarity. From *Colored Glassware of the Depression Era, Book II,* by Hazel Marie Weatherman.

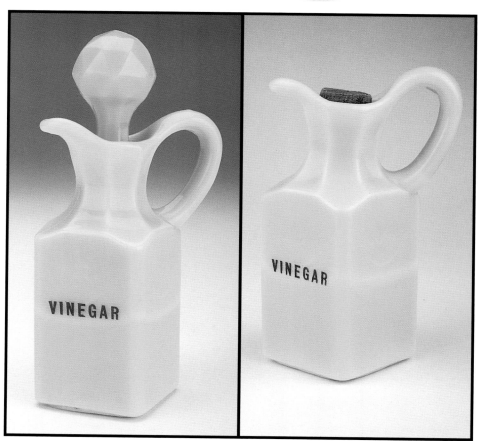

McKee vinegar cruet with stopper. Extremely rare. With stopper $1200–1500, without stopper $700–800.

Morgantown "Trudy" water bottle and tumbler set. This glass is noticeably thinner and more delicate than that of McKee or Jeannette. $100–125 set. Bottle alone, $45–50.

Jadite tumblers. Left: Jeannette bathroom tumbler was sold as part of the bathroom set, $80–90. Right: McKee tumbler, $40–50.

McKee tumbler with bear decal. $45–50.

Shot glass, 2 1/2",
$30–35. McKee
"Waldorf" egg
cup/footed
tumbler, $20–25.

McKee small
footed
tumbler with
floral band.
$18–20.

Light green ribbed
tumblers. $12–15
each.

Fired-on green
pitcher and tum-
blers. Juice pitcher
$40–45, tumblers
$8–15 each.

Vases and Flower Pots

A wide variety of jadite vases were produced by many glass companies. It is unfortunate that so few of them ever appear on the market. The concentric ringed bud vase made by the Jeannette Co. and the art deco vase produced by Anchor Hocking are the most commonly found and affordable jadite vases.

The McKee Glass Co. produced the widest variety of vases in jadite, with the "art nude" vase being highly sought after by jadite and art deco collectors alike. The cover for the smaller nude vase is scarce. We have been unable to locate documentation on this cover. No covers have been reported for the larger vase. The McKee "art dressed" vase is found much less frequently than the "art nude" vase. Although McKee Glass Co. catalogs list the availability of many more vases than we have pictured here, we have no way of knowing if all vases listed in the catalogs were indeed produced in jadite.

The Anchor Hocking flower pot with the scalloped rim is not as common as the plain rimmed pot. Notice the similarities between the vintage Akro Agate flower pots and the recently produced pots available through the Martha Stewart's *Martha By Mail*™ Catalog.

McKee large 11 1/2″ vase, $150–175.

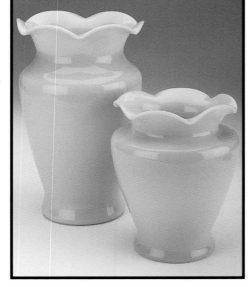

Above: McKee vases. From left: 6 5/8″ vase $100–125, 8″ ribbed vase $85–100, 4″ vase $65–75, 10 1/2″ vase $125–150, 6 1/2″ bulbous vase $100–125.

Right: McKee vases. 8″ vase $75–85, 11 1/2″ vase $125–150.

132

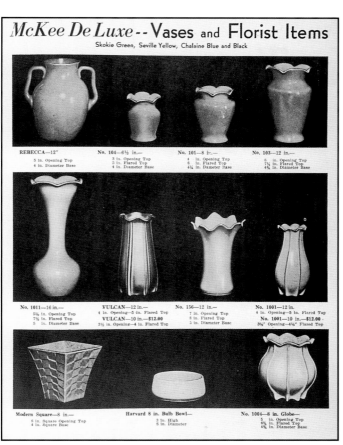

Page from McKee catalogue illustrating vases. Not all have been found in jadite.

Jadite 6" vase with ruffled top. $75–85.

Large jadite vase, 7" tall, 3-footed. $100–125.

Jadite vases. From left: 4 1/2" ruffled edge $75–85, 10 1/4" Morgantown vase $75–85, 6 1/4" ruffled edge $50–60.

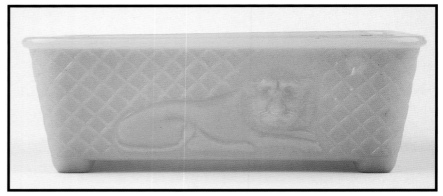

1931 McKee ad. From *Colored Glassware of the
Depression Era, Book II,* by Hazel Marie Weatherman.

Jadite 7 1/2" vase. $85–100.

McKee lion window box. $100–125.

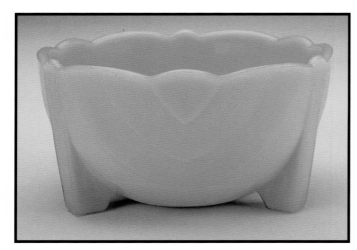

McKee 7" bulb bowl. $35–40.

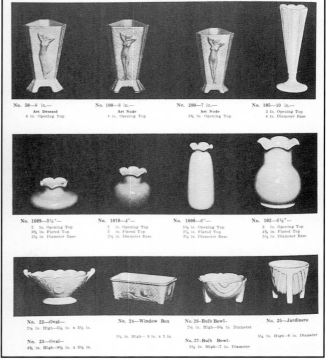

Page from McKee catalogue.

McKee vases. The nude vases are much more common than the dressed version. "Art Dressed" 8" vase $200–225, 7" "Art Nude" vase $150–175 (with cover $225–250), 8" "Art Nude" $150–175.

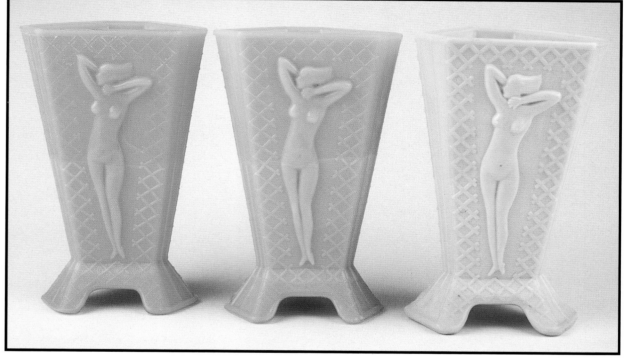

McKee "Art nude" 8" vases. Chaline $175–200, dark jadite $175–185, light jadite $150–175.

McKee 6"x11" centerpiece, $75–100. 10" vase, $100–125.

1931 McKee advertisement. From Colored Glassware of the Depression Era, Book II by Hazel Marie Weatherman.

135

Tall jadite vase.
$75–85.

Fire-king jadite 2" cactus pot. $50–60.

Fire-king vases. 7 3/4" tab-handled vase
$100–125, 5 1/4" deco vase $20–25.

Hand-painted 5 7/8" jadite vase. $50–60.

Jadite vases. Jeannette ribbed $20–25, McKee 6 5/8" $100–125, Fire-king deco $20–25.

Jeannette decorated ribbed vase next to plain leftover. Vase, $30–35.

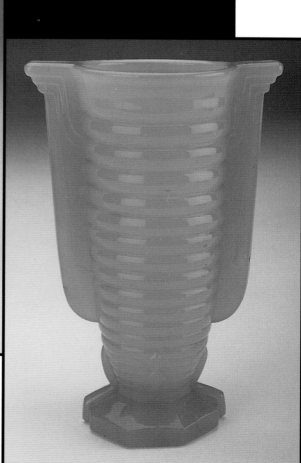

Clambroth 7 3/4" deco vase. $100–125.

Fire-king flower pots. 3 5/8" smooth top $20–22, 3 1/4" ruffled top $22–25.

Jadite flower pot. $40–50.

Fire-king fired-on green pineapple vase. $20–25.

Jadite flower pots. Left: 3 light jadite flower pots. Made by Fenton for Martha by Mail™, 1998. Right: 2 dark jadite Akro Agate vases, $12–15 each.

138

Additional Jadite

Despite our efforts to categorize pieces, some items simply have not fit into the sections we have created in this book. Others, like the Westmoreland pieces in this sections, are included here because they are jadite-like. They are included here to show the variety of items that exist and can be collected.

The candles are a recent creation by Mike Kury. They are entirely made of wax, but even up close they look like jadite pieces. They nicely compliment any jadite collection.

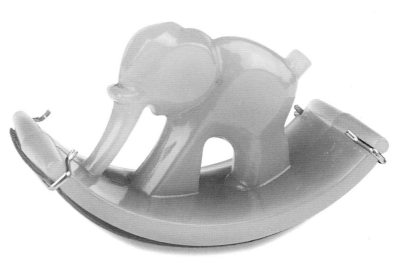

Above: Elephant ink blotter. Scarce. $100–125.

Left: Scottie Dog ink blotter. $40–50.

Small hand vase or toothpick. European. $30–35.

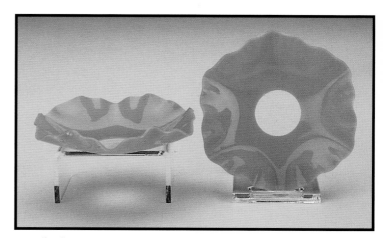

Candle drips. $15–20 each

139

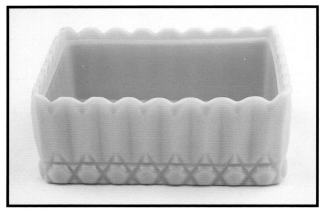

Above: Jadite box, 4" x 5". $30–35.

Right: Clambroth obelisk or wall vase. $100–150.

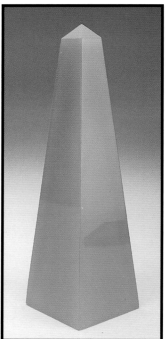

Above: Curtain tiebacks. $40–50 pair.

Left: Square shallow plate marked " China" on back, 7" across, darker than most Jadite. Unknown manufacturer and vintage. NV

Fired-on jadite pieces from the Anchor Hocking morgue. $15–20 each.

Grouping of clambroth pieces. $20–30 each.

Dark green bird feeder. $10–15.

Westmoreland hands tray. $25–30.

Westmoreland pitcher with white handle. $60–70.

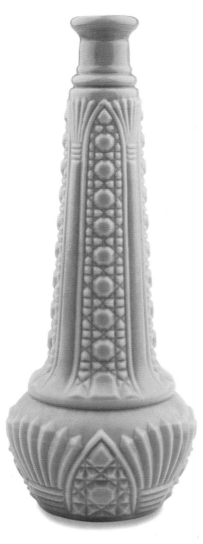

Top left: Westmoreland bottle or tall vase. $50–60.

Top right: Clambroth pieces. Sugar and creamer $25–30 set, candy dishes $15–20 each.

Lower left: Jadite go-along candles. These wonderful accessories are currently being made by Mike Kury. The cup and the vase are virtually identical to the Fire-king pieces.

Lower right: Westmoreland bottle with stopper. $60–70.

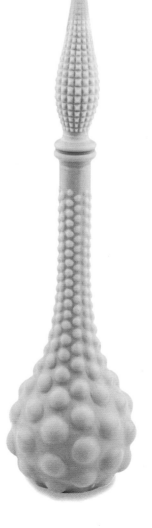

Martha Stewart

The current popularity of jadite kitchenware and dinnerware, at least partially, must be attributed to Martha Stewart's interest in the glassware. For more than a decade she has featured jadite in her cookbooks and decorating books. Her magazine, *Martha Stewart Living*™, has similarly focused on jadite in the collecting column. Her nationally syndicated television show has regular cooking segments with jadite-filled cabinets in the background. Similarly, most cooking ingredients in these segments are waiting in jadite bowls to be used in the recipes.

Her many uses of jadite in magazines and on television have pervaded popular consciousness. Antique dealers, shop staff, and customers at antique shows frequently refer to jadite as "Martha Stewart's green glass," much to the chagrin of many longtime jadite collectors. When questioned about this, we frequently find that these people don't exactly know where or how they have come to identify the glass with Martha Stewart. She is a popular culture phenomenon—she is a force that elicits sentiment and controversy. And while she is a four-letter word on one of the Internet chat groups pertaining to jadite, to others she is a guru of style. In either case, she is clearly a leading force in the jadite craze.

Martha's place in jadite history, however, was cemented most firmly when she recently commissioned Fenton Glass Co. to create a group of jadite accessory items. Many long term jadite collectors have voiced concern over the introduction of new and reproduction items into the marketplace; others are glad to add these items to their collections. These items warrant inclusion in this book, both to keep jadite collectors informed of what is in the marketplace and to let others know of pieces they can still acquire.

The quality of these new items varies. Certain items, like the tumblers and covered boxes, nicely compliment the older glassware. We find these items to be true to both the color and quality of the old glass. Closest to the McKee Skokie green, these items will both attract and confuse collectors. Other items, less likely to be confused with vintage jadite, are the beehive honey pot and covered turkey dish. They have an ornate, Victorian look and do not resemble most vintage jadite. The only pieces that truly are reproduction of vintage jadite pieces are the small flower pots. These are nearly identical to the Akro Agate pots.

There are several different markings used on these items, including "Martha by Mail," "MBM" and the Fenton "F." We have also seen pieces with no marking at all.

Above: Three sizes of cake plates. Sold individually and as a set. Retail prices: Set of 3 $149, small 6"x8" cake plate $49, medium 6"x10" cake plate $52, large 6"x12" cake plate $59.

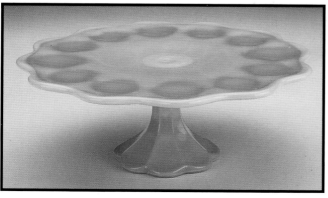

Left: Large cake plate. Looks a bit like a deviled-egg tray. Not very flat, 4 3/4" x 11". Retail price $48.

143

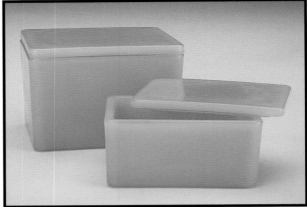

Covered boxes made by Fenton. Small box 2 1/2" x 3 1/2" x 4". Large box 3" x 3 1/2" x 5". Retail price $44 for the pair.

Covered turkey dish, 7" x 5" x 6 1/2". Marketed as a candy dish or individual soup tureen. Retail price $25. Covered jam dish or honey pot in the shape of a beehive. 2 3/4" x 4 3/4". Retail price $22. Small votive candleholder in the shape of a pail. 2 3/4" x 2 3/4" Retail price for set of 4, $32.

Set of four tumblers made by Fenton. Retail price $14 each or $48 for set of 4.

Three sizes of flower pots made by Fenton. Small 2 1/4" pots, retail price $28 for set of 4. Medium 3 3/8" pots, retail price $28 for set of 3. Large 4 1/4" pots, retail price $28 for set of 2.

Bibliography

Florence, Gene. *Anchor Hocking's Fire-king and More.* Paducah, Kentucky: Schroeder Publishing Co., Inc., 1998.

Florence, Gene. *Kichen Glassware of the Depression Years. Fifth Edition.* Paducah, Kentucky: Schroeder Publishing Co., Inc., 1995.

Kilgo, Garry and Dale, and Jerry and Gail Wilkins. *Anchor Hocking's Fire-King Glassware. Volume II.* Addison, Alabama: K.& W. Collectibles Publisher, 1997.

Measell, James and Berry Wiggins. *Great American Glass of the Roaring 20's and Depression Era.* Marietta, Ohio: The Glass Press, Inc., 1998.

Stout, Sandra McPhee. *The Complete Book of McKee Glass.* North Kansas City, MO: Trojan Press, 1974.

Weatherman, Hazel Marie. *Colored Glassware of the Depression Era, 2.* Springfield, MO: Weatherman Glassbooks, 1974.

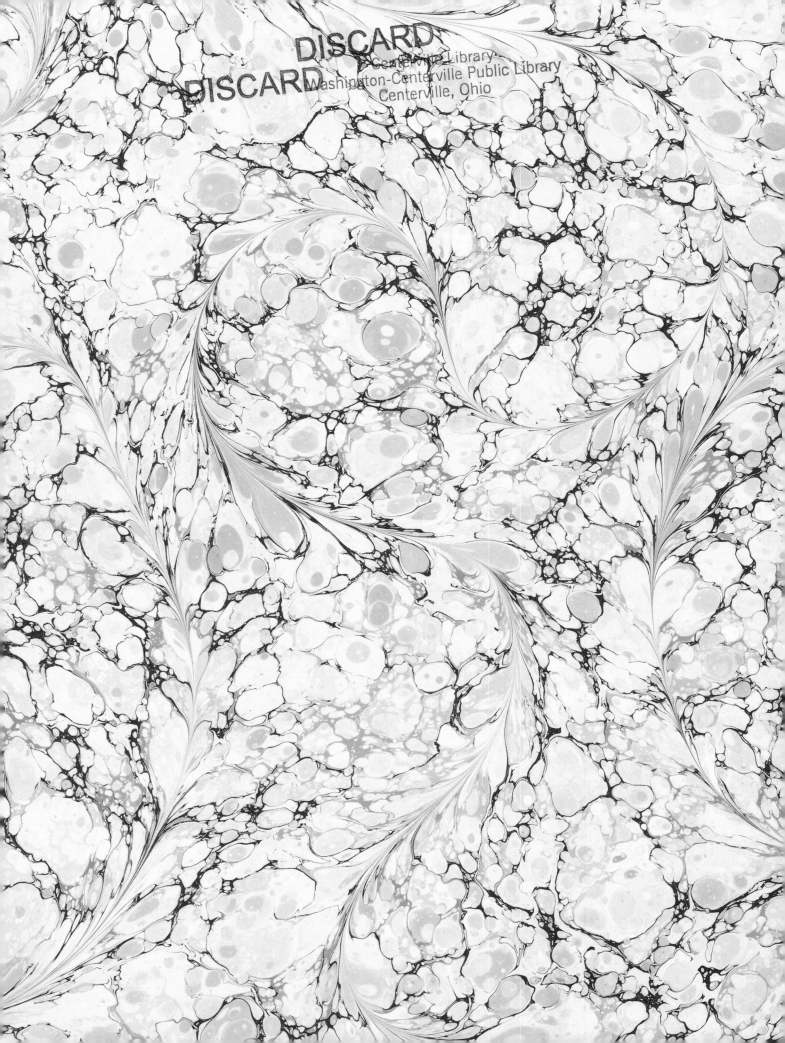